# Can you re

You bet, and Keith Johnson shows you how.

All across America, ordinary people earn good money keeping kids entertained and busy at birthday parties, family and corporate events, schools, festivals, restaurants and malls. While many perform full-time, others choose to work only on evenings and weekends, supplementing their incomes while having a blast at the same time. Sound like fun?

Think only a highly skilled magician, juggler or musician can make it in this business? Think again. A growing segment of family entertainers parlayed their hobbies or interests—jewelry making, baking, woodworking or you name it—into highly successful programs that kids love.

Filled with real-life examples and honest advice, *Make Money Entertaining Kids* gets you started in this fun and lucrative business.

---

*"By the end of the first chapter, I was already thinking of dozens of things I could do! I can't wait to get started."*
*—Ann Heiden, parent*

*"An upbeat, easy to read book that reads like it's talking to you!"*
*—Erin Kavanaugh, Puppets by Erin*

---

Featured in the September 1997 *Parents Magazine,* Keith Johnson has spent the last ten years proving that the ideas in this book work. Keith performs 500 shows a year at schools, libraries, malls and events throughout New England. He has written several books to motivate novice and experienced performers, including *Get Your Show on the Road, How to Create and Perform Routines for Family Audiences,* and *What Successful Performers Know.*

# How To Make Money Entertaining Kids

*—No Experience Necessary—*

## Keith M. Johnson

# COPYRIGHT NOTICES

How to Make Money Entertaining Kids by Keith Johnson

KMJ Educational Programs
25 Wildwood Ave.
Providence, RI 02907•(401) 781-6676
Keithbooks@aol.com (e-mail)

Johnson, Keith

How to Make Money Entertaining Kids/by Keith Johnson
ISBN 1-890833-05-3 trade paper
1. Entrepreneurship-Management. 2. Self-Employment-Management. 3. Hobby/How To

## NOTE

A small percentage of the content of this work has been synopsized from other books, reports, videos, cassettes and articles offered by the publisher.  If you would like more information concerning any of the topics contained herein, contact the publisher for a complete publications listing.

## LEGAL NOTICES

# Contents

# Introduction

So, you want to earn some extra money.

Who doesn't?

You want a job that will let you spend time with your kids. A work schedule that's flexible so you can work around your son's little league championship or daughter's dance recital. Or when a relative is free to baby-sit.

You want a job that won't leave you smelling like french fries, fending off drunks or peddling a plastic pop-top meat marinator to your friends and relatives.

In almost every city and town across the United States, and countries around the world, ordinary folks just like you are making hundreds of dollars each weekend. They are moms, dads, elementary school music teachers, grandparents, fire fighters, library aides, electrical engineers and college students. But in their free time, they double their weekday salaries, working for a couple of hours.

It's true.

How are they doing it?

That's what this book is all about. Helping you create your

own business, where you will enjoy flexible, family friendly hours and a creative outlet, In a business that allows you to earn extra money using skills you already have!

What do you do now for part-time work? A burger joint? Yard sale? Retail? Temp work in a stuffy office? How long does it take you to make $50? And do you have fun? This book shows you plenty of ways you can make $50 or more an hour, while having a blast with a group of kids.

Have fun!

Read through this book and discover what a great opportunity awaits you.

Happy reading! And good luck!

Best wishes!

*Keith M. Johnson*

# Chapter 1 • Fun Money!

Many people wonder how much a kids' entertainer makes a year. Sometimes they ask me in a pitying sort of way what I do for a "real job."

Don't feel sorry for me.

Last year, I made over $120,000.

This is my "real job." All I do is entertain. I make good money by keeping kids busy and entertained at parties, events, schools, restaurants and at popular tourist destinations. When you are done reading this book, you will know exactly how I make my fun money. Then, you can get started just like I did. I hope you will. It's a whole lot easier to do than you might imagine!

I know someone who happily earns $85 an hour by entertaining kids. What does she do that commands such a high fee? What are her awesome skills? She offers an hour long "Princess Party" for little girls.

*That's it?* I hear you ask. Yes, that's it. She wears a

shiny pink dress and a glittery tiara, helps the kids make princess cone hats out of colored paper, tells (reads) fairy tales, plays princess games like London Bridge, and finishes with a formal tea (juice poured from a tea pot into a plastic tea cup set). For this she makes $85 an hour, and she has more work than she can handle. She won't take more than five or six parties a weekend.

Who else do I know?

An appraiser who, in his spare time, makes $60+ an hour leading games at corporate summer picnics and family included business conferences at area hotels. All the same games you played in grade school—red light green light, water balloon toss, pin the tail on the donkey, pinatas, sack races, musical chairs, and dodge ball. He used to do these games at birthday parties too, but party parents only want him for an hour or two. Corporations want him for four or five hours at a time.

Then there is the secretary who does school and library presentations about how she makes it through the day with the help of her seeing-eye dog. She donates her $50 to a foundation established to help more people discover the joy of service dogs.

Or take the cash strapped mom who bends balloons at a family restaurant three times a week. Two evenings and Sunday brunch. She hops from table to table, making balloon creatures for tips. She earns between $40 and $80 each day, depending on how busy the restaurant is. In two or three hours! It took her less time than that to learn how to make the eight basic shapes. It all started with an instruction book from the library, a bag of balloons from the party supply store and a bicycle pump.

There are lots of people who do loads of different things to keep kids busy and entertained. And you can be one of them! This book is written in three parts. All will help you get started entertaining kids for fun and profit. The first section will give you insider advice on where the work is, and the kinds of shows that sell. The second section offers secrets that successful performers know—tips that will help you develop great shows! The final section includes down to earth business advice to get you started. Throughout the book, I've sprinkled stories about entertainers who are working—both full and part time—and making money. Let them inspire you.

You can make money in your spare time, just like they do.

# Part One • Finding Your Niche

# Chapter 2 • The Qualities of a Successful Entertainer

I've been in this business for ten years, and I've met a number of entertainers. Many excellent performers choose to work part-time while others rely on this business to support their families—it's a full-time job. Regardless of whether they work full time or part time, all of the good entertainers I've met have these qualities in common.

## They like kids

If you really don't like kids, forget about entertaining them. Kids will forgive you a lot of mistakes but if you genuinely dislike them, they will tear you apart. I've seen it happen and it's an ugly sight. No amount of faking a tolerance for them will help. If you understand and appreciate what makes kids tick, and care enough to do activities they will like, you will prosper. Otherwise, expect a mob of children to locate your hot buttons and push them with glee, just to watch you dissolve and fizzle away.

If you're in it just for the money, you will get your comeuppance too. Kids can tell when they are being used.

## They know their "audience" and provide appropriate activities

Once I saw a performer get hooted, red-faced, off the stage by a riotous pack of fifth and sixth graders. Those kids were just fine with the previous performer but something about this guy got under their skin. It was probably that he treated them like *kindergartners*.

The audience's jeering started after a flip warning was issued by the performer. The threat went something like this, "If you don't all sit quietly, like good little girls and boys, right this very minute, I'm going to pack up my puppets and go." Kids can recognize an easy out when they see one.

**Getting under their skin**

MIKE GEORGE / THE SUN CHRONICLE

Keith M. Johnson, at right, of Providence shows children at Vogel School in Wrentham a snake skin, part of his presentation "Science Isn't Always Pretty." The program was presented by Fiske Public Library and sponsored by the Sweatt Fund.

*Knowing your audience, and keeping them involved in your program, is a hallmark of a good entertainer.*

Here's what I suggest. Put yourself in the kids' shoes and peer through their eyes, especially as you are putting your activities together. Develop a program or activity which hits them at their level. Kindergartners will get frustrated if you play games with difficult rules. Third graders are beyond finger-painting.

## They involve the kids

The best way to keep kids interested in your entertainment is to get them participating in it. If you are applying tattoos, talk to the children and let them choose which picture they would like. If you are doing a show with a science theme for preschoolers, use assistants from the audience to help in the experiments. Participation is a key to success in this business.

## They work for the person who signs their check

Your job is to make the adults happy by providing appropriate activities for the kids. This is just as true for a school show performer with two hundred kids in the audience as it is for the balloon bender with an audience of one.

If you choose to make the kids happy by getting them wound up—starting a battle of balloon swords or teaching them naughty songs—you are not going to last long in this business. You've got to make the adults happy too.

## They build variety into their act

Game leaders at birthday parties soon realize that a continuous string of similar games will bore the kids. Stringing beads to make a necklace is fun for just so long. Tea parties need more than just tea.

A change of pace will help hold the kids attention. If you offer animal petting areas, a hundred bunnies will not attract as much attention as an area with some bunnies, a parrot, an iguana, goats and a pot bellied pig. If you are running a do it yourself tie-dye table at the Elks community social, have tee shirts, big boxer shorts and bandannas to choose from. In my school show about American History, the characters I feature range from Pedro Flores (the immigrant who brought yo yos to America) to Deborah Sampson (the only known female soldier of the American Revolutionary War).

## They have a game plan

Kid show entertainers must be prepared. "Winging it" leads to serious trouble.

When you start fumbling around for what to do next, you lose momentum and the attention of the kids will wander. If you lose their attention, the children start misbehaving and then it's a struggle to get them back into line. A well planned presentation or activity is a key to crowd control.

## They enjoy the experience

Successful entertainers choose to do activities that they enjoy also. How else would someone come up with a "Tool Time" woodworking theme party? This woman loves woodworking. She brings the tools and supplies for the kids to make jewelry boxes, bird feeders, pine wood derby cars or fantasy pieces. She has a great time showing the kids how to glue, nail, saw, measure, paint, sand and clean up.

Remember, you will be doing this same presentation or activity over and over—I sometimes do four or five performances of the same show each day! In order for you to be fresh every time, you must do things you personally enjoy. And then you must find the venues where that act works best. In the next chapter, we will take a look at the different venues available to entertainers.

# Chapter 3 • Where's the Work?

Let's take a look at the "big four" venues available to kids entertainers. Each venue has its own demands. They hire for different reasons. As you read, think about where you could fit in based on your interests. It will depend on what kinds of activities you want to do, when your free time is and what age group you want to work with.

## Parties

Can you really get paid to party?

You bet! It's one of the easiest ways to make fun money.

These are usually smallish birthday parties for three year olds on up through ten or eleven year olds. Sleep over parties and family get-togethers (such as baptisms, reunions and anniversaries) hire entertainers too. These parties are generally held on weekends between eleven in the morning and

*You don't have to be a skilled magician, juggler or clown to make it on the "living room circuit". Your own skills and interests will make for a great party business.*

five in the afternoon. However, in recent years I've seen a small trend toward scheduling kids' parties after school and in the early evening. Parties typically have seven to fifteen guests.

Party entertainers are hired to keep the kids busy from a half hour after the guests arrive until it's time to open presents or eat the cake. Rarely will you be asked to stay longer than fifty minutes to an hour.

Typically, parents look for entertainers who can keep the kids busy with party games, themed activities (a tea party, GI Joe adventure party, or jewelry making party, for instance) or they hire someone who will do a whole "show". Don't worry if you're not a highly skilled clown, puppeteer, juggler or magician. If you can paint faces, run a bingo for little prizes

*Mrs. G. turned her love of arts and crafts into great birthday entertainment. What do you love to do?*

or organize a sack race, that's good enough for a lot of parents.

Most entertainers start out doing parties because they are easy to get, pay well, and you can use very simple activities to keep the kids busy.

## Events

I've lumped a great many venues into this category.

Think back to all the times you have seen entertainers at work. Malls, Christmas parties, parks, zoos, neighborhood cook outs, alumni weekends, parades, museums, fund-raisers, street festivals, the list goes on and on. Wherever groups of kids gather and need to be entertained, someone is at work. Why not you?

From the clown who hands out balloons at a sidewalk sale to the person who mans the church picnic craft activity table—people are making money keeping kids busy. Your only limit is your imagination! Don't worry if you don't have any "skills" at the moment. You're probably selling yourself short. Almost everyone has skills that can translate into viable entertainment. And there are plenty of simple things you can learn to do in very little time. I know someone who taught himself to walk on stilts. One summer he made a pair of very long legged pants, spread on some clown make up and volunteered to "walk around" during his kid's summer camp's Olympic day. He carried a feather duster and "dusted" the tops of people's heads for a couple of hours. He was such a hit that now I run into him all the time at events all over the state. He still dusts heads, but now he makes $125 an hour.

Later when we discuss the many activities you might choose to do, picture yourself working for these events. They can be great fun, and profitable.

## Schools

Preschools, elementary schools and libraries regularly hire

entertainers. They look for topic driven presentations that will add to their students' educational experience. Do you know a lot about the history of your town? Are you a volunteer fire fighter, bagpipe player or the owner of a unique pet? Have you sailed to distant islands, camped out in the tundra or met someone famous? Do you care about environmental issues, reptiles, art, baseball, nutrition, literacy or math? Do you know the difference between a T-Rex and a T-Bird? Think about what excites you. If you can speak passionately about it, you can make a wonderfully colorful presentation.

*Here I am performing I FEEL GOOD! one of my five educational programs. I perform at over 200 schools and libraries each year.*

By engaging the imaginations of students, you teach them something without them even realizing it.

Because you can "speak from the heart", some entertainers find these the easiest kind of presentations to create. And, they pay really well. The going rate for a forty five minute elementary school presentation in New England starts at $250.

## <u>Working for tips</u>

Here's how to get paid to have a blast with kids, even if your schedule is unpredictable. You can arrange with local restaurants, movie theatres and stores to entertain there whenever your calendar allows. You develop a short one-on-one skill—such as face painting or balloon twisting—and you work for the customers who are shopping at the store, standing in line or waiting for a table. This is called "busking", and many entertainers do nothing else! Most kid-oriented shops and restaurants are happy to work with a "busker" because buskers work for tips. You are given a tip of a dollar or two whenever you paint a face or twist a balloon. The store or restaurant essentially gets your services for free. Therefore, they are often happy to have you outside their store to attract attention and foot traffic. Even if yours is not a regular appearance, they are likely to say, "Come back when ever you get the chance!"

## A "BONUS" fifth market

This one doesn't quite fit as one of the four venues—because it has little to do with kids. But it is worth mentioning because it's one of the ways I paid the rent when I was just out of college and starting my business.

## Nursing homes and retirement communities

Senior centers, nursing homes and retirement communities are always looking for activities and performers to entertain their residents. If you sing, juggle, play an instrument, or tell jokes that someone over 80 won't find offensive, this is an excellent market, especially if you are available midweek to do your programs. When I was just starting out, I sat down with the yellow pages and called every nursing home in my state. I talked to the activity director, and three or four of them booked my show—each week. Performing these shows gave me lots of experience in standing up in front of an audience, dealing with interruptions (such as the time when a man stopped my show to call out "Nurse, Nurse, I gotta go to the 'terlet' Nurse!"), and working with clients. This is a very easy market to get into very cheaply. What could you do to earn extra $100 or $150 a week?  Could you perform at three or four retirement homes, helping a  group of your elders laugh, cry or sing?  Think about it.

Now that you have an overview of the different ways you can make money by keeping kids busy or entertained, let's take a closer look at each of the venues and the type of shows that are appropriate for them.

# Chapter 4 • Starting out— parties and small events

*You don't need to be an "expert" to entertain at parties!*

Listen to the sounds coming from living rooms and backyards all around you. The squeals of delight as a child opens the perfect gift, the laughter as they hear a silly joke, and the screams of joy as they successfully finish their very own craft project. And what else are these kids doing? CELEBRATING A BIRTHDAY! Kids see birthdays as a way of confirming that they are special. And what better way to celebrate than with a super-duper birthday party?

Imagine taking an hour

out of your schedule to help make a child's birthday truly memorable. Imagine helping him celebrate his unique existence on this planet. And best of all, imagine getting paid $50 to $150 for the pleasure.

Lots of parties happen on weekends, holidays, summer days, after school and right after dinner on school nights. So whether you have a full-time job but need extra income, or you're an at home parent who needs money, you can fit this business into your life-style. Would an hour or two or even three out of the day, a couple of days a week, cut into your plans too much? Probably not.

The great thing about this business is that you choose which parties to accept and which to refuse. It's a job where you don't have to beg for time off just to see your son or daughter play in the city sports finals. If you need a weekend off, you just turn down shows for that time period. No problem!

## Why those parents need you

Your job is to give the parents a rest. Make no mistake about it. This is the real reason you will be earning good money. Many adults would rather not entertain kids in their spare time. Even their own child. So they hire somebody to do it for them.

Parents frantically search for someone who can take charge of a chunk of time in the middle of their child's 2-3 hour long party. They are afraid that they will not be able to control the guests' behavior for such a long stretch of time. They don't have the time or experience to plan activities to keep the kids busy. They are panicked because those kids are going to rip their house apart if there are no programmed activities. That's where you come in! By making parents' lives easier, you quickly earn a reputation on the living room circuit! And a good "rep" means that you'll be able to increase your fees, and do more shows!

# Events

After a while on the "living room circuit", your program of activities becomes so polished that someone will ask you to entertain at their *event*.  It may be a small festival, a women's club picnic, church social or a corporate family holiday party.

At events, you are not going to be the main focus.  Usually, you are one of many things happening during the day to keep the kids busy and entertained.  Events are not a whole lot different from parties.  They are crazier, with more people in attendance.  You may be asked to do your thing for multiple hours or at various times during the day.  Events pay more money than birthdays.  But, all in all, events usually just feel like big birthdays.  There's more running around, but at your activity the kids participate and react just as at small parties.  And that's a good thing.  The transition is a smooth one.

Birthday parties and small events are an excellent way to "cut your teeth" and gain experience in the entertainment business.  Many performers love these venues so much, it's all they do!  It's not hard to develop a program that will be competitive in this market.  Why?  Three reasons:

- There are lots of kids having parties.
- Parents welcome (and even compete to find) a program that is different.
- It's easy to advertise your business cheaply and effectively.

# Chapter 5 • Working for Tips

Working for tips is called "busking." When you think of performers you have seen busking, you may think of a musician or juggler who performs on a street corner with a hat placed on the ground to collect spare change. There is more to it than that—you don't have to stand on a street corner anymore! Many family friendly restaurants, shops and businesses welcome buskers because it draws crowds and attracts attention. Let me explain.

For a couple of years I worked at a Mexican style family restaurant. They let me make balloon animals for the kids at the restaurant during peak family dinner hours in the midweek and at Sunday brunch. My pay came in the form of tips from the parents. The restaurant didn't cut me a check but they did cut me a deal. An open invitation. Each week I'd give them a call and we'd set up a schedule. It was a great deal for both of us. They got great word of mouth advertising as a "kid friendly restaurant" and the services of an entertainer whom they couldn't afford to hire on a regular basis. I earned between $40 and $100 for two or three hours work, during slack times when I hadn't booked regular gigs! I passed out a lot of business cards too, which resulted in more paying jobs. And frequently, they gave me a free dinner.

When you busk, you should do something fun, short and one-on-one with the kids. Something you can make for them or do for them that takes a minute or two and makes them feel like they got an individual show or service. Balloon sculpting, face painting, caricatures, magic tricks, that sort of thing. Because buskers work for tips, they have to do something that will inspire individual adults to pry open their wallets and dig out a dollar. Individually entertaining their child, showing them a great time for a short while, usually is enough to rate a buck or two from the parent. This is especially true if you wear an "I WORK FOR TIP$." badge. That lets the parent know if they don't want to tip, they should discourage their children from getting in line to get their faces painted.

Busking isn't limited to big cities. Look around in your town for opportunities. What businesses in your area cater to kids or to the parents of kids? That's the question you need to ask yourself. Look for opportunities where kids will be with their parents and the parents will be spending money on something else. Public playgrounds in small cities have plenty of kids but not an atmosphere where parents will spend money. Shopping centers and malls having back to school sales will have the kids and the money spending parents. Other good busking sites include: the sidewalk outside a popular ice-cream store on a hot summer's night, the theater ticket line an hour before a new Disney movie is starting, a busy corner with lots of tourist foot traffic, a beach or public pool, a kids' activity center featuring games, mini golf and pizza, a busy family restaurant, even parades, local festivals and holiday street parties.

You need to get permission to work in these settings,

but if you present your case in a way that makes the business feel like they are getting something for nothing, you should win them over. What do they get? They get customers who will linger longer and are thus likely to spend more money. You will be a magnet to lure more customers to the establishment. People will go home and talk about the establishment and tell their friends about the fun time they had. Your antics will energize the atmosphere and entertain many more people than just those you "work" for. If the business or venue doesn't like what you do, after you try it out, they can ask you not to come back with no hard feelings.

Busking is a way for you to get work without having to advertise. You're not sitting around waiting for the phone to ring, instead, you're advertising your services in a way that pays off big time. You earn quick cash, and you hand out a lot of cards to people who will call you in the future! Size up the situation and if it looks like you could make some money, ask for a try out. The results are immediate and usually lots of fun. Plus, you set your own hours and you might just find a venue that will offer an open invitation to you.

In the next chapter, we'll take a look at the different activities and skills that you could develop into a busking routine, a party program or a full-fledged show. As you read the next chapter, think about your life experience and hobbies. Is there a show inside you?

# Chapter 6 • Activities and presentations for parties, busking and events

Think this might be a good business for you, but unsure of what you would do to entertain a group of kids?  Read on.  This chapter is full of ideas to get you started.

The difference between activities and presentations is sometimes a gray area, as you will see.

Generally, *activities* keep the kids busy and entertained because they are fun things to *do*.  They involve creation, play, cooperation or individual tasks.  Activities work best at parties or events.  Mural painting areas, bean bag toss games and pie eating contests are activities.

*Presentations* keep the kids busy and entertained by giving them something fun and engaging to *see*.  Presentations include puppet shows, balloon sculpting, makeup (cosmetic) parties, the wonderful world of magnets, cartoon-alongs or any type of demonstration.  School shows and buskers are almost always presentational. Parties and events welcome presentations, but you must offer a high degree of audience participation.

If you mix *activities with presentations,* the result is usually a *learn along* or *do along with me* activity. When you lead a mass aerobatics class for kids gathered at the mall for the Healthy Kids Week Celebration, you are presenting and they are participating in the activity.

Kids enjoy learn along activities. Teaching juggling, painting techniques, paper making, paper bag puppet making, star gazing, cooking, fossil hunting, butterfly identification, the physics of toys, these are all things that kids would like to "see and do."

If someone offered you $50 to come and keep their kids entertained for an hour at a party, tomorrow, could you do it? Sure you could. An "entertainer" is hired to keep the kids busy and happy at parties and events. You don't have to do shows. Take a look at how simple and straight forward these entertaining activities can be.

## Games leader

Party games, tag games, skill games, games of chance, team games, individual games, trivia games, sports, rhyming games, singing games, brain teasers, food games, indoor games, outdoor games, toss and catch games, hiding games, memory games, blindfold games, racing games, talking games, silly games (make a mummy, wrap your friend in toilet-paper), board games. Games are traditionally the best way to keep a group of kids busy and entertained at parties and events.

Kids enjoy playing games so much that sometimes they need a leader to do little more than provide a winning prize and tell them <u>what</u> to play <u>when</u>.

## Arts and crafts

There's something about a creative project that will keep most kids, young and old, absorbed for a long time. Kids

*Crafts, like this beading party, are very popular these days.*

like to use their imaginations and their hands. Add in materials that are colorful and fun to manipulate and you have a winning crafts activity. Pipe cleaner sculptures, wearable art, drawings for the fridge, mixed media mobiles, button art, puppet making, weaving, play clay, tin rubbing, soap carving, pressing flowers between layers of wax paper, clay that you shape and bake or microwave to make your own beads, jewelry, collages, junk art designs, paper mache monsters, paintable painters' caps, ray guns and robots from paper tubes, and the list goes on.

You can string a number of craft activities together to keep kids busy and entertained for a longer amount of time. Or, with a single five minute activity, you can serve many more kids at an event with your craft activity table.

Most crafts are self directed activities. Once you teach them the basics, the kids entertain themselves. And when the craft no longer seems fun, they move themselves on to another activity. Even then the fruit of their effort remains and is a tangible keepsake or gift to take home after the event or party.

How simple can this be? A friend of mine gets paid to tack up long lengths of paper. I'm talking about those four foot wide rolls of white paper that many facilities use to cover their dining tables. He tacks twenty foot long sheets to walls or fences or lies them on the ground and the kids create huge murals by coloring them with paint, markers or crayons. They color in huge pictures he sketches on the paper. Sometimes they just doodle, graffiti or make life sized self portraits by lying on the paper and outlining themselves. If it's a birthday party, the result is rolled up as a gigantic birthday card. The kids love this.

## Activity stations

Fun play stations are another easy way to keep kids busy and entertained without needing any performance skill at all. Why couldn't you offer a menu of activity station options for your sponsor to select from?

Science experiments or collections of cool stuff to see and try make for easy to offer activity areas. Provide magnets and bits of metal and encourage kids to explore the wonders of magnetism. How about covering a table with fossils, Barbies™ and outfits, animal pelts, collections of rocks and minerals or motors, wires, batteries, buzzers, flashlight batteries and switches? What if you bought up a whole bunch of used Tinker Toy™ or Lego™ sets at yard sales and put all the bits and pieces in a shallow plastic kiddie pool for kids to play with? You could be the Lego™ lady!

I've been to fairs and festivals where one entertainer is hired to provide a "bubble" station. The bubbleologist brings five or eight large 5 gallon buckets half filled with home made bubble solution. He also provides an assortment of odd shaped bubble making tools and equipment for the kids to fiddle with. This is a simple station that solves of a lot of problems for the party host or event planner.

For many reasons, many parents and planners would rather pay someone to run the station than do it themselves. They don't have to think it through, buy the stuff or find volunteers to manage the station. Plus, hiring a professional means it will be a more entertaining experience. The bubbleologist can anticipate and prepare for problems that a first timer would never think of. Chances are, that bubble pro will roll up his sleeves and demonstrate some wild bubble blowing.

Is there a bubble gal or guy in your area? If not, how hard would it be to become one? That's *fun* money.

## Silly stunts

Teach kids how to hang three spoons from their face or make paper helicopters. Coach hula hoops, peacock feather balancing or make incredible growing trees from rolled up newspapers. Kids will think you are amazing. Make a shrill whistle out of an acorn cap. These and many more stunts await the silly stunt-thrill seeker in all of us. Do it for the kids! Silly Stuntman rides again!

*Your interests can earn you money!*

## Face painting, fortune telling, removable tattoos

These sorts of activities, especially the face painting, are extremely popular ways to amuse kids. Kids younger than 7 generally like face painting. Between 5 and 10 they like the removable tattoos. Older than that, a silly/mock fortune teller will engage their interest. These experiences leave kids feeling like they have had their own little, personal "show" for three to five minutes.

## Make overs, fashion don'ts and hairdos

This is a recent entry into the living room and sleepover party circuits. If you have a flair for doing and talking beauty secrets, this is right up your alley. You're invited to a party to "do" the young ladies' nails, hair and face. Perhaps you might determine their "colors", give wardrobe style suggestions and recommend accessories. Share beauty secrets. Show them how to work that lipstick, blush and mascara or nail polish. You can add a touch of class to the party! Along with a touch of green to your purse.

## Skills and hobbies

Many parents have found that the best person to invite to their 8 year old's party is a high school kid who plays a sport. That high schooler teaches the kids a few soccer skills (or you name the sport) and then organizes a game. The kids love it, especially since someone as cool as a high schooler is there doing the teaching.

There are barrels of hobbies and skills you could share with kids at a party. You could do fashion design, rocketry, coin or stamp collecting, gardening, writing, animal care, puppetry, history, aerobic dancing. Give them a chance to sample something fun at their own pace. Give them a taste of a hobby that gives you lots of satisfaction and fun.

*Another excellent idea of parlaying your interests into a fun party!*

## Presentations

As I said, kids like to see and do cool things. Presentations involve seeing cool demonstrations or displays. You can demonstrate almost anything. A yo-yo. Or how to decorate a cake. Or how to play the oboe. If you can make your skill interesting to kids, you will find a market for your presentation.

What if you have a collection of authentic Indian artifacts? A presentation where you tell stories and pass the artifacts around for examination would thrill the kids.

# Walk around costumed characters

If you buy a large dinosaur suit—you can be a "Dinoguy for hire" and stroll around glad handing kids and posing for photos.

Characters like large rabbits at Easter, Santa for Christmas, and others are big hits at events all over the country. In recent years, "Purple Dinosaurs", "Adolescent Turtles" and "Big Yellow Birds" have packed a big entertainment wallop at parties and events. Famous cartoon, book, and television characters are protected by trademark laws, and corporate lawyers have been known to crack down on people who use the character for profit without paying licensing fees. If you want to perform as The Purple Dinosaur or Yellow Bird, consult your lawyer for advice first. I recommend creating your own distinct, fuzzy character.

**Pony Rides**

for
- Birthday Parties
- School Fairs
- Company Outings
- Family Days

*Available all year*

**Paul's Pony Parties**

*Has your child outgrown his pony? Put the little guy to work!*

## Animals

Reptiles, bugs, birds, fish, etc are great guests at a party or event. You give the kids a chance to meet, learn about and enjoy the antics of our feathered, furry, scaly, slithery friends. From pony rides to nature lectures, animals are a popular activity.

## Story telling

Puppets tell stories, music can tell stories, movement can tell stories, art, even magic tricks can be used to bring stories to life.

Go to see storytellers of all kinds whenever you can. Drop in at story hours at the library or bookstore. You will see

*We've come a long way from the days of "pin the tail on the donkey." While traditional parties are still popular, specialized parties represent a growing niche in the market.*

the kids transformed and transported. If that seems like a nice thing to be able to do for kids, maybe you will work a little storytelling into your program too.

Don't think you can memorize a story? Parents have been known to hire story *readers* for their kids parties.

## Clown skits

A painted face, big shoes and colored hair are not required to do clown antics. But they don't hurt the presentation. There are many books that will show you how to use big, colorful, silly props to make kids laugh. Visit a costume supply store, magic shop or gag shop and see what you can work into your program.

## Art

Kids love the "magic of art", which is creating something out of nothing. Watching a

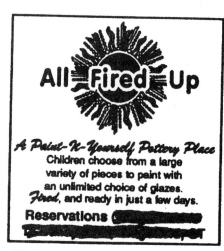

*Kids love to make things. And this party teaches them basic art skills, too!*

picture take shape on a sheet of paper really is fascinating. Turning a mound of clay into a recognizable animal is truly engaging.

## Puppets

Kids (especially those younger than 8) love puppets and puppet shows. Generally, puppets are used to animate stories and bring them to life. Kids look upon the most humble finger puppet as an independent living thing.

You can use store bought figures so there is no need to create your own. Bring extra puppets so the kids can act out parts of your story.

## Crazy skills

Can you juggle, yo-yo, pogo, stilt walk, ride a unicycle, do incredible Frisbee stunts, tumble, balance on your hands or toss a top? What ever your skill along these lines, you can use it to entertain kids.

## Balloon sculpting

I talk a lot about balloon bending as a perfect activity for kids' events, for a number of reasons. People like to watch the sculptures take shape. You can give them away. The are big and

*Have you spent most of your life acquiring useless skills? Me too, but I turned them into a business. So did Mike the Hatman. So can you!*

*This woman turned her Volkswagen Bus into a Party Prop—complete with "dress up" clothes from the sixties. Do you suppose she also brings her Grateful Dead 8-tracks?*

colorful. And, they are really easy to learn how to do, cheap to produce and the act of making them is a '"show" in itself. You don't need to learn any acting or "presentation" skills.

## Stories about your adventures or occupation

Do you have an exciting job that would fascinate and captivate kids? Are you a soldier, policewoman, construction worker or dog trainer? Take a look at the things you've done in your life. Kids love to hear storeis and see the "stuff" of interesting experiences. Do you compost earthworms? Collect 70's memoribilia? Were you on the Olympic bicycling team? Show kids your bike, helmet and all the stuff of professional "biker" has to have in order to achieve the competitive edge. Share your interesting experiences. Kids love it!

## Music

If you can play an instrument, sing or write music,

*This is just one of the many ways you can entertain with music. Do you play an instrument or sing? There may be a show inside you, too!*

then you can encourage others to sing and play music to the best of their abilities. If music is your muse, you've got it made. Music is a large part of the growing up experience and makes the stuff of interesting activities. There's music to move to (Itsy Bitsy Spider), and music that tells stories (She'll be Coming 'Round the Mountain). Music to calm (lullabies). Music is also part of games (musical chairs), and gives direction (Ring Around the Rosie); musiccan help celebrate (Happy Birthday) and gives us a means to express ourselves (kids can tap alon with tambourines and rhythm sticks.) Music can be used in so many ways to entertain and educate. It's a natural for family events.

# Chapter 7 • School Show Know How

As you hone your skills, and focus on the things that interest you the most, you'll find that many venues open up to you. You may also find that you enjoy motivating kids to do something as much as you enjoy entertaining them. That was my experience, and it's the experience of many other performers I know. Let me take a minute to share my story with you.

As a teenager, I taught myself how to juggle and do simple magic tricks. Since I already had those skills, I decided to make money by entertaining kids as a juggling magician and balloon sculptor. After a year or two of working parties and events I decided it would be good to break into the school market as well. This was in the mid 1980's. What I discovered though, was that shows that were "just for fun" were no longer acceptable in New England's schools. The principal and PTA leaders were looking for educational content and curriculum based themes. Performances needed to reinforce what the teachers were doing in their classrooms. A juggling and magic based comedy show wasn't going to do the trick.

It's still the same way today. In fact, many states now have laws that regulate the content of enrichment programming.

Rather than complaining that I couldn't get work as a juggling magician, I changed my course a bit and developed a program with an educational theme. Sure, some of my shows now have a juggling or magic trick in them, but they also carry an important message that ties in with what kids learn at school. Educational shows are now my specialty. Though I still do my share of events and shows just for fun, the lion's share of my income comes from school shows. These days, I work at over 200 schools, libraries and museums every year. I've written five educational shows and none of them features more than a smattering of my circus skills. I could put any one of my educational shows "on you" in under a month, whether you have performing experience or not. (But I don't offer this service, so please don't call to ask.)

Each of my "humor based educational programs" supports a particular element of kindergarten through sixth grade curriculum. With titles such as *Science Isn't Always Pretty!*, *Amazing Americans* and *Let's Talk Trash*, I have something good to offer nearly any school. I work hard to meet their yearly enrichment objectives. The same goes for libraries and museums.

It takes me about two years to create each show and get it up and running smoothly—this is partly because I do thorough research, and partly because I have to schedule this "creative" time around my busy performing calendar.

I start out by determining a hot topic, researching, gathering interesting props and information, scripting, testing, advertising and finalizing the performance and content. That makes it sound like a very difficult process. I can also describe the process of getting a show up and running like this. . .

# I Feel Good!

The human body is an incredible machine. In I FEEL GOOD, Keith motivates students to make positive choices for healthy living every day. Using the Food Guide Pyramid (the shape that keeps you in shape) and aerobic body science demonstrations, I FEEL GOOD teaches three simple things we can do to live better: Eating smart, exercising regularly, and trying hard to be our best.

## Let's Talk TRASH

Dr. Trashman needs your help! Journey with him from the peaks of a landfill to the depths of the ocean. Together, Dr. Trashman and your students search for the answer to the question, "What can we do to help keep our planet healthy and clean?" Using current scientific data (not propaganda), humor, and assistance from the audience, our uncommon hero makes the 3 "R's" of ecology crystal clear.

---

# Science
## ISN'T ALWAYS PRETTY

What makes a scientist tick? Is slime a liquid or a solid? And does it fly? What (or whom) do owls eat for lunch? The answers are in SCIENCE ISN'T ALWAYS PRETTY.

Your students will witness Keith break the sound barrier with a machine which travels over 760 miles per hour, and watch one enlightened student light a bulb with the power in his bare hands.

Science is the study of why stuff happens and how things work. This show uses elements from your science curriculum (e.g. gravity, machines, energy, physical reactions and the food chain) in outrageous and fascinating ways. Your students learn that science surrounds them and influences everything they do! Keith's best-seller!

---

balls fly through the air. Classic children's literature collides with a modern game show. This irreverent and rousing pep rally transforms every week into a reading week. By reading everything from road signs to classic literature, your students will learn that reading is power. You'll love HATS OFF TO READING.

Look to

### Keith M. Johnson

for
- Humor-Based Education
- Curriculum-Based Programs
- Competitive Fees
- Great Support Materials
- Audience Participation

## Amazing Americans

Take a fantastic trip through our nation's past and meet some extra-ordinary people who used their unique gifts to change our world. Meet George Washington Carver, the incredible Revolutionary War patriot Deborah Sampson, Pedro Florez, and other immigrants who helped shape our country. Integrating your history curriculum, reading, and audience participation, this show celebrates invention, diversity, hard work and perseverance.

---

# HATS OFF TO Reading

Adventure, mystery, comedy. Reading takes students to places they've never been before, and encourages them to dream great dreams. Silly animal poems leap to life while juggling

---

*This is a copy of my 1996-97 school show brochure. Over the years, I've developed five different educational programs for the school and library market.*

**IMAGINATION CONCERTS!**
Singing, dancing, imagination, stuffed animals, puppets, 100% participation - ages 1-8

**"WORLD PEACE-THE CHILDREN'S DREAM"** Concerts
ELEMENTARY SCHOOLS
Participation concert of music celebrating
Self-Esteem, Diversity, The Earth, World Peace

**Cheryl Melody Productions**
B.M.Ed.; M.A. - Recording Artist, Performer, Music Educator
"Come with me on a musical journey, and together
we will sing, dance, laugh and imagine the impossible."

*Cheryl takes two interests, music and world peace, and combines them into one educational program.*

I look for a topic the schools will buy, but I only develop the topic if it's personally interesting to me. I dig into the subject and if I find it fascinating, I will proceed. Research is done in many forms including: field trips, interviewing interesting experts, buying cool stuff which is related to the subject, (which will become props for the show), reading topic centered children's books and current literature. After the research phase, I choose the one thing I'd like the room full of kids to remember about the subject when my show is over. Writing the script is easy when I keep that "one main point" in mind.

I focus on including exciting and colorful material, props and information that the kids will be able to identify with. My intent is to come across as a really cool guy who cares deeply about the subject of the show. Kids, parents, teachers, and principals all respond to that as much as they do to the factual content. I include lots of audience participation in the form of mock game shows, audience assistants and question and answer periods. All of this I squeeze into a forty five minute presentation which I test, for free, at local schools until I've worked out the bugs. Then, I offer the show in the next round of brochures that I send out to the schools. A trickle of interest soon becomes a steady flow due to word of mouth and regular advertising. I take six months to a year off (from writing) to clear my head. Then it's time to write another. That's my "process".

I hope you will consider creating your own educational program. Kids need to experience more presenters who are truly captivated by the topic they are talking about. Too often, they see teacher types as detached and compassion-free reporters of events, facts and figures. Trust me, students wake up and warm up to learning when it is enthusiastically presented.

# Chapter 8 • School Show Performers & Styles

What kinds of people do shows for schools, libraries and museums, and what kinds of shows do they do? We start with the one category of presenter I think most of you will fall into.

## Ordinary folks

*I truly believe that anyone who truly likes kids can make them care about an educational topic.* I'm not only thinking of senior citizens, firemen, librarians, teachers, coaches, preachers or parents. Some of the most

**NATURE & NURTURE**
Environmental Educational Programs
• primitive survival skills
• geology • snake adventure
• eew, worms! • creepy crawlies
• pond exploration • under the sea
• animal tracks & signs
*Fairs/ Festivals, Schools, Birthdays, Libraries, Camps*

*Wildlife, particularly reptiles, are also very popular in the educational markets.*

engaging school shows I've ever seen were presented by "regular people" with no arts or performing experience and not even any formal training or study of their topic. They were simply excited about sharing a subject they had learned a lot about (self taught) and were passionate about sharing. Their show was usually tied into a hobby or a subject they had been interested in for a long time. That sustained interest gave them the aura of an expert.

How about you? What are you interested in? What could you share with kids that would enrich and compliment their studies?

Examples:

**MICHAEL GRAHAM'S**
SPRING VALLEY PUPPET THEATER
PRESENTS

### THE THREE WISHES

What would you do is a magical Elf gave YOU three wishes? That's just what happens to Henry and Gretchen in the puppet production of "The Three Wishes".
This folktale favorite is flavored with a dash of dialogue, a generous helping of humor and the twists of plot for which the SPRING VALLEY PUPPET THEATER is known.

—— and ——

### THE WOLF IN SHEEP'S CLOTHING

A hungry Wolf tries to outwit the savvy Sheperd and make a meal of the helpless little Lamb. But is she?
Adapted from the Aesop fable this popular tale is enlivened with a colorful Mexican setting, a humorous communication gap and a surprise ending!

BOTH STORIES FEATURE BEAUTIFULLY CRAFTED HANPUPPETS AND COLORFUL SCENIC DESIGN. THE PROGRAM RUNS 35 MINUTES. FOR AGES 5 AND UP

*Interested in puppets? Bringing traditional stories to life for the early elementary grades may be for you.*

Meet Ben Franklin. He was surprised that his grandkids had never heard of the wonderful life of Ben Franklin, so in 1993, Mr. Lund, then 63 years old, decided to do something about that. Now, he dresses like Franklin and talks with groups of kids (as Franklin himself did) about invention, hard work, travel, fun and the meaning of 1776. He encourages the kids to ask questions, and answers them as Franklin.

*A professionally trained juggler, Henry Lappen is a naturalist for fun. He's turned this hobby into a very popular school program.*

China. The Land, its people, and why some Chinese people come to America. This is a fascinating look at modern immigration issues, from a real true blue immigrant's point of view. Mrs. Chang has been an American citizen for ten years. She brings with her a fresh perspective on a sometimes confusing and challenging issue.

Betty Loves Numbers! Betty's always loved numbers and she see them everywhere! Find out where numbers came from, how they developed and where we would be without them. In Texas, this show supports second and third grade curriculum!

What other types of presenters are there? Take a look.

## **Performing artists**

These are dancers, musicians, singers, mimes, storytellers, actors, puppeteers, vaudevillians, magicians, jugglers, clowns. People who have trained to present an entertaining and engaging skill. Examples:

Jo Ha Performance Group. A delightful journey into ancient Japanese court culture with its elegant dance, *bugaku*, with sumptuous costumes and exotic music.

Mallory Bagwell is a mime/movement artist who explores

the roots of communication through words, gesture, intonation, facial expression, body language and more.

Gideon Freudmann, Cello-Bop uses humor and a friendly approachable manner to teach you everything you will ever want to know about the cello.

## Visual artists

Include authors, painters, quilters, sculptors and photographers. They usually provide educational workshops and hands on learning experiences. These craftspeople express their thoughts through their artistic creations.

Examples:

John Buller. A children's author/illustrator, tours to schools and presents assemblies about his process of creating books.

Annette Leroux. A textile artist/weaver who demonstrates her craft and teaches the history of the textile business in America including pre and post industrial revolution.

## Professionals

Work experience often makes for a natural educational tie in. How does what you do now connect with what kids study in elementary school?

Examples:

Come Fly With Me. An astronaut talks about how math kept her safe in the shuttle.

A fire fighter presents a fire safety program and demonstrations, exhibits his equipment and talks of life in a fire station. That's fire safety and civics.

A retired police detective offers SCIENCE INVESTIGATIONS: Investigate a live crime scene and use the clues to solve the Mr. Bear mystery. It explores physical and life science.

## Call him inspiration on wheels

These days, Kit Summers is riding high — a long way from his 37 days in a coma after a truck hit him. Summers, the author of "Learning with Finesse," now gives talks on setting goals, turning challenge into opportunity and breaking barriers. On Thursday, he visited St. Joseph School in Collingdale, where he juggled and did magic with help from first grader Gloria Radico and third grader Michael Loughran.

For The Inquirer / JAY GORODETZER

*Kit Summers uses his personal experiences to motivate his audience. His remarkable recovery is a powerful story that captivates students and adults.*

## People with unique life experiences

Here, the educational element sometimes takes a back seat to character development issues. Extraordinary individuals, or ordinary individuals who do extraordinary things, can encourage the best in all of us. Kids included. So, what's *your* story?

For instance:

Elliot Washington is fighting back from accidental injury. He uses a slide show and talks the kids through his injury and recovery.

Angie Riveras who rose above the mean streets to become a successful business person. Kids on field trips visit her manufacturing plant. The plant is located in the inner city and employs residents of surrounding neighborhoods. Ms. Riveras talks about her youth and her awesome turning point.

Ongassa Bloomanthol, an American Eskimo who trekked across the African continent and brought back plenty to see and touch and hear. She uses lots of stories to contrast how she grew up as opposed to how the kids in Africa grow up. A real learning experience.

# Organizations

Institutions often provide public education (outreach) programs. Historical societies, museums, heart associations, scouting councils, crisis centers, dairy councils, etc usually offer these programs. They make presentations/lectures/workshops available to interested groups. These programs advance the organization's mission, to educate the public and create an interest in their cause.

*The New Canaan Nature Center offers these natural science events for schools and parties.*

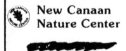
Professional actors might be hired or a volunteer is called upon to deliver the presentation. The dairy council hires two performers to be a talking and dancing cow to preach the glories of milk.

DARE officers in the schools are supported through police and local business resources. Both have a big stake in drug free kids.

In Worcester, Massachusetts, Higgins Armory Museum has touring outreach programs on arms, armor and life in ancient Greece and Rome, the Middle Ages and Renaissance.

SAVE THE BAY, a non profit eco-oriented organization in Rhode Island has volunteers who tour schools and events to discuss the problems of pollution and preserving wildlife areas.

# Chapter 9 • Choosing Your Path

Now that your head is full of ideas on what you could be doing, how can you learn what kind of entertainers are making money in your community? One of the quickest ways to jumpstart your entertainment career is to "go to school" on those folks who have already made it in the market you are attempting to break into. Stealing what they do is strictly forbidden. There is no faster way to make enemies and drive yourself out of business. Rather, look at the sorts of activities your competitors offer, for what ages, in what venues, how they advertise, what their price is and how they position themselves as a unique product. You can be sure that the successful entertainers have made many mistakes while developing their programs. By studying what they do you can hopefully avoid some of those mistakes.

## Know who is, and who is not, your competition

David Copperfield gets lots of work and does a great magic show, but he is probably not your competition.

Copperfield does shows that work well in large theaters, for an audience who likes to go to the theater. If you dream of working in those venues, this book can get you started, but you've got a long road ahead of you. However, if you're looking for performers who do great programs for audiences in schools, festivals, libraries, parks, living rooms and church basements, you will learn quite a bit about the business in your community.

Your competition is not only entertainers who have the same skills as you. If you are a clown, other clowns are not your *only* competition. Magicians, balloon artists, storytellers, reptile presenters, even jewelry making theme parties—everyone who is competing for the jobs you are interested in is your competition.

## Finding your competition

If you're going to do educational shows, talk to librarians and elementary school parents group members. Ask to see their files of brochures. Question them about entertainers they have had and what they thought about them. Go to see the performers when ever possible. If you are trying to break into the party, event or busking markets, scour the yellow pages, classified advertisements, shopper bulletin boards and anywhere else your competition advertises. Once you have done that, you should have a pretty good idea who you're up against. The hardest competition to peg will be those entertainers in your area who work with agencies and party planners, though they usually promote themselves outside the agency as well.

## What you are looking to learn

1. You can see what sort of program material "flies" with that specific audience you're after. Are your customers looking for technical prowess or silly antics?
2. You will get a sense of the price range your market

has. This will give you a clue as to what you should charge.

3. You get to see where the successful performers advertise their services so you will not waste money placing ads in the wrong place. Veterans don't waste money advertising in bad places.

4. Listen closely, and you'll hear key words repeated by various competitors. If you expect to get work, you'll need to offer these services, or have a compelling reason to be different. In New England, birthday customers want to hear: audience participation, 50 minutes to an hour, birthday child is singled out, balloons for every kid and I'm happy to perform outside.

5. Performers often list many of the particular venues that they have worked in the past. Since you know those places hire entertainment like yours, you can add them to your mailing list.

6. Look for add-ons. Do the school show performers offer post-show classroom visits or teachers guides? Does your party competition offer to bring goody bags, will they stay late to play games or will they paint faces for an extra fee? Do the sidewalk sale entertainers send a picture of themselves so the mall can use them in promotions? If they can do it, so can you.

7. How do they bill their clients? Do they require contracts, a deposit, or written directions? Do they charge travel, offer some sort of guarantee? Do they hold dates for a week or will they only pencil you into a date if you book right now? If it's a picnic or outdoor party, do you still have to pay them if it's rained out?

8. Does your competition use answering machines or is there someone who answers the phone? Do they return calls for information promptly? Were they confident and courteous on the phone or blustery and impatient? Good customer service might give you an edge over poor service skills.

9. Can you get a sense of how far ahead they are booking and what are the busiest times of their busiest days?

10. Do they offer references? Give them a call and find

out. Call your competition and pretend to be shopping around. If they do have references, call the reference to see if their story matches what the performer says she does. If they don't offer references, ask why. Their response should be very revealing.

I bet you can see now why I'm such a firm believer in studying your competition. It increases the chances of your making the right move rather than stumbling around blind in your efforts to promote your program.

# Part 2 • Trade Secrets to Help You Act Like a Pro

# Chapter 10 • The Power of Themes

After you've decided which skills or activities you'd like to include in your program, it's time to figure out how to link all of the pieces together. Here's one secret weapon that many entertainers don't use—because they are too lazy. You should use it. It's a winner.

*Parties and events that interest boys are harder to find. This is a popular party event with elementary school-aged boys (and girls!)*

Creating a program around a theme is a trick that most entertainers adopt only after years of experience. This one tip is worth ten times the

> **KID'S TOOL-TIME Parties:** For ages 6 and up. Wooden projects constructed by your child and friends, while introducing them to the tools of the trade. Call ██████████

cost of this book—so read carefully!

When people are shopping around for an entertainer for their party or event, they soon realize that lots of entertainers do the same thing. So how do you stand out in the crowd? Since you are just starting out, you probably don't have impressive credentials or any references. An exciting theme and program name will distinguish your offerings.

A game leader who provides an hour of indoor or outdoor games is nice. A gameleader who offers the same program, but calls it "Monster Olympics" will get more work. My point is simple. What ever activities you choose to present, try to build them into a theme and then create a catchy title.

Why offer a generic tea party when an American Girl Tea Party would be more exciting? Calling yours an Animal Art Party is more descriptive than

Art Activities. Grandpa's Good Old Fashioned Birthday Party Games sounds like fun.

Take a look at the entertainers' ads that are scattered throughout this book. The truly engaging ones are selling an experience not just activities. The

*The Swat Team is an imaginative theme. It creates a strong image.*

title and theme will help those hiring you to imagine what it is you offer. The theme and title will create a mental picture in their heads. The picture will help them decide to hire you over another entertainer who offers similar activities. They can imagine the kids having a blast playing zany monster games. They know their kid's friends will look forward to anything to do with the American Girls theme.

Sell a memorable experience not just a collection of activities.

# Chapter 11 • Making Money with "Edutainment"

Edutainment is a relatively new entry into the kids entertainment market. Entertainers at parties, events and schools are wise to continue adding edutainment to their programs, because sponsors and parents warm to these programs, and book them readily.

## What is edutainment?

In the old days, sponsors looked for shows that would either entertain or educate, depending on their needs. Now they look for a combination of the two. Like it or not, kids watch a lot of television and they expect everything in their lives to be as entertaining and engaging as *Sesame Street* or *Bill Nye the Science Guy*. As a result, entertaining shows that deal with an educational issue or theme sell like blazes. Camps, malls, even birthday parties seek out programs that work some sort of learning experience into the act.

Another factor in the trend toward edutainment is that

# Teacher uses humor to turn yucks into yuks

Keith Johnson makes learning fun.

Often, when people hear topics like eating well, reading and recycling, they assume the subject matter is educational and, therefore, "dull" and "dreary."

Certainly not entertaining.

"That's the mold I'm trying to break. Humor is a good teaching tool," Johnson said.

After one of his comic/educational shows, teachers frequently ask Johnson about using humor in their lessons.

"It's just a way of thinking," he said, adding that "it doesn't take a comedian to see humor in different situations."

In fact, Johnson describes himself as a quiet, unassuming introvert. "I'm not a particularly funny person."

For the past decade, Johnson has touted his one-man show to elementary schools, libraries, fairs, festivals and corporate events in New England. His repertoire includes "good, solid family humor" and old-fashioned fun.

"I call myself family entertainment. Many shows adults enjoy it as much as the kids, or else I'm not doing my job," he said. "I enjoy learning educational stuff. I get motivated and excited about what I've learned and I want to share my

**PATRICIA A. RUSSELL**

enthusiasm with others to make learning come alive and exciting for them."

He has a trademark outfit: khaki beige pants, blue shirt, tie and tennis sneakers. "It's a funny outfit," said Johnson.

Using curriculum-based topics such as physical science, environmental issues, American history and reading, the performer's fast-paced show gets everyone involved with and excited about learning.

The non-stop action includes keeping the children involved.

"Make bunny ears. Eyeglasses up. Eyeglasses down. Blow under your armpits. Arms up. Arms down. Round of applause," Johnson instructs, adding, "Can I recycle my sister into a new sister?"

His "Round of Applause" routine is incorporated many times throughout each of his shows.

"It's sort of become my stage mark," he said.

Labeled a slow learner in grade school, Johnson believes his real problem was that he didn't read well. To help him, his mother made him read out loud every day.

He also was lucky enough to receive help from a dedicated and humorous special education teacher, he said.

"I picked up a lot of skills when I was young," he said, including teaching himself to juggle — now part of his routine.

His first job was a jester for medieval banquets. That's how he found out he could entertain. His hobby turned into a vocation.

He earned a BFA — bachelor-of fun arts — from a three-month stint with the Ringling Bros., Barnum & Bailey Circus Clown College in Florida. He later received a real bachelor of arts from Roger Williams College in Rhode Island, where he studied dance, theater and children's literature.

Last year he was selected as a touring performing artist for the Bushnell Theater in Hartford.

Johnson's "Hats Off to Reading" program features the performer reading silly animal poems, wacky game shows and juggling high jinks. He reads "The Ostrich" by Ogden Nash, "The Purple Cow" by Gelett Burgess and "Mice Are Nice" by Rose Fryleman.

"It's my poetry in motion," he explained. The show's message is simple: reading will take you places.

"Hats Off to Reading" will be presented at the Mansfield Public Library, 225 Hope St., Mansfield, during spring vacation week on April 17 at 2 p.m. Reservations are necessary for this free event by calling (508) 261-7380.

"Johnson combines magic and poetry and stories. He's a great entertainer. That's why we're having him back," said Janet Campbell, children's librarian.

"Does low fat milk come from cows who are on diets?" Johnson said, introducing his latest show: "I Feel Good."

Its message: "It's your body, it's your job to take care of it."

The Stoughton Public Library will host "I Feel Good" April 18 at 10:30 a.m. at 84 Park St., Stoughton. Call for reservations at (617) 344-2711. This Sunday the performer will be featured at WSNE Kids' Fair at the Providence Convention Center in downtown Providence at 12:15 and 3:30 p.m.

Admission to the Fair is $6 for adults and $3 for children. Johnson's "Just For the Fun of It" features a variety show for kids and parents.

*This is a press clip that explains more about my edu-tainment programs.*

*The Parrot Lady teaches kids to respect animals in her edu-tainment program*

parents want their kids to have the best opportunities. Their kids must be better and smarter. So parents buy expensive educational toys and enroll their kids in afterschool enrichment classes. They limit television viewing to PBS and other educational stations. These parents are often looking for an quasi-educational component to every aspect of life—including parties and events. That's Edutainment!

## How can you take advantage of edutainment?

I read about "the Parrot Lady" in the paper recently.

*Music with a theme makes for another excellent example of "edutainment."*

She does programs for schools and parties. She travels with two or three semi-trained parrots. Kids learn about the birds—what they eat, where they come from, how they are cared for, etc. They get to hold the birds. Then the birds do a small show based on revealing the bird's natural behaviors.

Obviously, the Parrot Lady loves her birds, and wants to help others discover how wonderful they are. Do you have a hobby, skill or profession that kids would like to learn about? If you do, you too can be in the business of edutainment.

For instance, if you are a fire fighter, you could bring your uniform and some of your equipment to events to let kids try it on and to tell them stories about life in the fire house.

If you're a creative tightwad who likes to create arts and crafts out of household garbage, teach your hobby to kids. They can work alongside of you as you make sculptures, collages or jewelry out of "trash" such as milk jugs, orange juice lids, old magazines and scrap paper. Work in a message about keeping the earth clean by making less trash and you have an edutaining activity.

Magicians can follow their magic show with a workshop where the kids learn how to do a trick or two.

A storyteller who is interested

*Another example of how animals can be used to teach important skills and lessons.*

Interactive Programs for Birthdays and Schools

**Shows Include:**
- Reptiles • Amphibians
- Birds • Bugs
- and assorted Mammals
  *Our hands-on presentations teach respect and appreciation for exotic and unusual animals*

USDA Licensed • Insured

in the environment can theme his stories around rain forests or endangered species. Or if you're interested in America's heritage, you could tell stories representing the different waves of immigration.

*A desire to teach kids about the environment led to the development of this program, hosted by Mr. T. aka Jack Golden.*

Game leaders can lead games that teach cooperative skills rather than fostering competition.

Edutainment is one of those trends that wise entertainers will incorporate into their programs. It's a way to set yourself apart from your competition. And it may be your ticket to getting started in larger venues, such as libraries, schools and museums. That means more work (and more money) for you!

BORN in Lancashire, England, Joan trained as an elementary school teacher specializing in English Literature and Music. She taught in England and Quebec, Canada, before settling in Rhode Island where she is now a full-time storyteller.

JOAN performs for children, adults & families at schools, libraries, family celebrations, fund-raisers, parties, & festivals.

*Joan Bailey is an excellent story teller, and her British accent adds immeasureably to her program.*

To arrange a storytelling event on your choice of subject or theme, contact:

# Juggler shows pyramids kids can eat from

By Ange'e Carter
Register Staff

BRANFORD — When most people think of a pyramid, they think of the royal tombs of ancient Egypt, which are considered one of the Seven Wonders of the World.

But to Keith M. Johnson, a pyramid is the shape that keeps us in shape.

Johnson, a resident of Providence, R.I., came to town recently to introduce John B. Sliney School students to the Food Guide Pyramid, an illustrated chart that teaches the nutrients provided by each of the food groups.

"It's built bigger at the bottom and smaller at the top, just like the ancient pyramids in Egypt, right?" Johnson asked a group of about 200 students.

"Right," they answered in unison.

Pictured on the bottom row of the pyramid were drawings of bread, rice, cereal and pasta, the carbohydrates that give us energy. Johnson said.

"You need to start off the day with eating that stuff," he said.

Other rows showed vegetables and fruits, which are good sources of vitamins and minerals; dairy and meat products, which are rich in calcium; and the "tippity top" was empty.

"There's no food at the top of the food guide pyramid. The stuff that goes there is stuff you shouldn't eat a lot of every day, but only as a treat. Do you know what those foods are?," Johnson said.

The youngsters had lots of answers for that category. "Candy ... cake ... cookies ... chocolate ... soda," they yelled.

Students and teachers were quite tickled when Johnson said, "I read in a scientific magazine that soda is the No. 1 cause of belching in America."

Johnson's humorous lesson included a juggling demonstration to emphasize low-impact aerobics and the need to dedicate time every day to reaching your goals.

"It's your life. It's your body. You've got to take care of yourself. If you're able to stay with something, you'll get more out of it," Johnson said.

He is a graduate of the Ringling Bros. Clown College in Florida and Roger Williams University in Rhode Island. Johnson is self-employed and performed 525 juggling and magic shows last year at New England elementary schools, libraries and museums.

*Here's another clip from one of my shows. This one explains I FEEL GOOD, my show about personal empowerment, fitness and nutrition for grades K-6.*

**How to Make Money Entertaining Kids   63**

# Chapter 12 • Show and Tell

I'm going to let you in on a secret. It's a trick you can use to create an program, even if you have no previous performing experience. I've seen this method work over and over again. It is called *Show & Tell*.

Remember back in preschool or kindergarten when it was your turn to bring something into the class and share it with the group? You stood and without hesitation spoke naturally and with enthusiasm. It was easy to be animated and passionate because that object you were sharing meant a lot to you. (Was it a vacation photo, your favorite stuffed animal or a prized birthday gift from grandpa?) Don't you wish putting together a show could be that easy now? It can be, if you're willing to incorporate the lessons you learned from show and tell.

## What you learned from show and tell

1. Talk about something you know and care about. *That made you an undisputed expert among your classmates and gave*

*you confidence.*

2. Bring something for the audience to look at. *You won't feel everyone's eyes on you, if you give them something else to focus on.*

3. Avoid big words and fancy concepts. *Use words your audience can easily understand.*

## Show and tell was fun!

You followed the simple rules. You didn't suffer from stage fright or stumble over words. You told an interesting story, and shared a few facts and personal feelings about something. You were an expert; everyone was quiet and listened to you. The confidence and energy you radiated as the object was passed around is what held your audience spellbound. They asked questions that were easy to answer, because you knew your stuff. It was magic. For a few minutes you gave a group of kids something interesting to see and something colorful to hear. You were in control. It was so simple.

That's what I do nearly every day.

I'm a successful school show performer because I choose subjects that truly interest me and then I speak passionately about them. I give hundreds of kids at a time something interesting to see and hear plus multiple opportunities to participate in the show. I take the time, beforehand, to make sure what I present will truly be relevant and engaging to my audience. That way, they willingly pay attention and want to cooperate. In other words—I don't spend lots of time dealing with troublemakers or glossing over boring stuff. Neither should you.

## An example

I FEEL GOOD! is my show about personal empowerment, fitness and nutrition. I perform it for kindergarten through sixth grade students. In it, I *show* lots of stuff and *tell* lots of interesting things which are relevant to the health and well-being of those kids in the audience.

## What I show

During the show, I use the following: a plastic skeleton, a skull with a brain, a huge 6 foot food guide pyramid loaded with life sized realistic looking foam food, a cymbal to crash, a short juggling routine, a game show with three volunteers from the audience, an aerobic exercise performed by audience volunteers, and a coordination test for the kids in the audience.

## Some things I tell

During the show, I reinforce a few simple concepts: It's your life, your body and your job to learn how to take care of yourself. I help kids learn that you eat with your brain (not just with your mouth). That it's important to turn on your mind, and turn off the TV. That I was in fifth grade before I could read as well as the rest of my classmates, but that I didn't give up until I could read well. That I was a special ed. student, who graduated from college with honors. And that I taught myself to juggle by reading books in the library. The final thought I leave them with is this: it's important to try hard to be your best everyday—not just once in a while.

## The message

The goal of my show is to leave the kids with one simple thought they can carry forward and act upon. In I FEEL GOOD, the message is this: As they make their way through life, their own *behavior* will impact their health, happiness and success more than any other factors.

## Fine Tuning the show

As I research a topic, reading books and magazines and talking to experts, I constantly ask myself questions. What props can I use to capture the kids' attention and create lasting visual images?  What words and phrases should I use to communicate these important issues to kids who are in kindergarten through sixth grade?  How can I make them care about the subject enough to change their own behaviors?

That last question, about changing behavior, takes the development of the show one step beyond the show and tell method.  Changing behavior requires a *call to action.*

## Call to action

With a call to action, we go one step beyond simply showing and telling.  Instead of just showing and telling, you will show, tell and inspire!  You will encourage the kids to learn something more, try something new, do something right or simply pay more attention to how they feel about your subject.

In every one of my programs I strive first to get the kids interested in the subject, then to care about the subject and how it impacts their lives.  Then, when they realize they care about the subject, I call them to action.  Each show has a different call to action.  *Amazing Americans* challenges kids to learn more about the history of their own families.  *Let's Talk Trash* encourages them to do simple things in order to keep our world a little cleaner.  *Hats Off to Reading* motivates students to use their ability to read to teach themselves more about the things they are interested in that are not covered in school.

If you can build momentum in your program, a call to action will be honestly regarded by the audience and will cap your show perfectly.  If your program fails to stir their interest and curiosity, a call to action will be met with resistance.

Educational programs can be as easy as show and tell.  I hope my secret inspires you to get up and get started.

And keep in mind that while my shows are just like

show and tell, there are two big differences:

    1. The "class" I'm standing in front of is usually 200 students strong.

    2. I get a nice check after I return to my seat at the end of my presentation.

## Other entertainers who show and tell

There are many ordinary people who make a career out of doing show and tell. Here are just a few. As you read these, think about your life experiences. What would you do for show and tell?

*Fred Myers* is the Chairman of the science department of Farmington High School and a Connecticut recipient of the 1990 Presidential Award for Excellence in Science Teaching and many other honors and awards. His program is called PHYSICS FOR THE FAMILY IS FUN!—This presentation centers around everyone's intuitive grasp of the fundamental laws of physics. Many vivid demonstrations and interesting questions add excitement to this science program. (60-90 minutes)

*Rob Taylor*, mountaineer and storyteller performs a program called THE BREACH—Taylor shows slides and recounts his near-fatal climb of Mt. Kilimanjaro, Tanzania. An argument with his partner shifts the story from adventure to self-discovery, relationships, self-reliance, peer pressure, faith, friendship, and the realization of the potential we all hold within, which is the message of *The Breach*.

*Marla Novia*, also known as The Snack Lady has been conducting her theatrical Nutrition Program throughout Connecticut schools for the last 13 years, working with grades Pre-K—6. Using a light hearted, fun approach, bundles of cool food and her motto, "Nutrition Can Be Delicious," she shows the children how much fun it can be to bypass "junk food" in favor of the "help your body grow" foods. Her program and philosophy have attracted national attention, including The New York Times. The main discussion deals with dietary considerations, body fat, and blood cholesterol levels in relation to human well-being.

# Chapter 13 • Working with Audience Assistants

Another obstacle I hear when I talk to would-be performers is a fear that disruptive kids will come up on stage and ruin the fun. You should not let this stop you from succeeding as a performer. As I've said before, unless you really hate kids, you can learn to manage them for an hour or so with a performance, activity, or game. Yes, some kids are brats. But most brats are simply looking for rules. If you set the rules in advance, and quickly and fairly enforce them, you will do just fine. And there are many good reasons to include audience volunteers in your shows.

Audience volunteers add depth and color to your program and activities. It doesn't matter whether you are a busker, school show, party or event performer. Including assistants from the audience is important to the success of your offerings.

The Golden Rule applies to your use of volunteers: Treat them as you would want to be treated, with compassion, respect, and attentiveness. The other kids, out there in the audience, are living vicariously through your assistant. Treat your assistants well and you will be a hero. Treat them badly, and you're a heal.

Planning is critical when choosing a volunteer. Consider these points when adding audience involvement to your program.

## Pick the right kid

Trouble starts when you choose a kid who is incapable of doing what needs to be done. You know what tasks they will have to accomplish, take your time and select the right kid for the job. Pick her ahead of time, in your mind.

In my science program, SCIENCE ISN'T ALWAYS PRETTY, we dissect an owl pellet—a regurgitated lump of last night's leftovers—bones, fur, skull etc. I use an assistant to hold the paper plate under my hands to catch the stuff that falls.

*This youngster is a perfect volunteer. The look on her face as we disect the owl pellet is pricelss!*

Keith M. Johnson dissects an owl pellet with the help of audience member Lindsay Tremblay, a second-grader. Johnson tells the children that scientists can tell everything about an animal by studying these. This particular pellet contains the remains of a mouse, yellow teeth and all.

I also ask her a lot of questions about what kind of bone she imagines we're finding, what kind of animal it came from, and so forth. But her real job is to be grossed out. Her facial expressions and the "yechy" sounds she makes add a neat dimension to the show. Therefore, I try to pick a nicely dressed second grader with a big smile and a true eagerness to help. She adds immeasurably to the presentation by being herself.

## Pick an average kid

Don't pick kids who are extra poorly or fancily dressed. Don't pick the kid who is screaming "pick me!" the loudest. Don't pick the kid who is crying because he didn't get picked last time. Don't pick the kid who is jumping out of his place the highest, or a kid who was overtly rude earlier in the program. Don't pick a kid with a dull look in her eyes. Pick a confident, well-behaved kid. That kid should have the right stuff.

## Other kids notice the assistants you choose

Those who want to be picked will try to act like the kids you did pick, so pick nice kids. Some presenters go so far as to say, "Bobby, I picked you to help because you were sitting there so nicely and you looked like you wanted to help."

## Have everything ready before your assistant arrives

Prepare the activity and then invite an assistant to help you. They will get nervous if you leave them standing on stage as you fumble around trying to set up your next activity.

## Welcome your volunteer

He may not be comfortable in front of a crowd. Welcome him warmly. This will go a long way toward getting the most out of him. A quick and easy question or two is appropriate. What's your name? Have you been on stage before? What grade are you in? Do you take the bus or carry your homework to school?

## Treat your volunteer with respect

They are not your foil, they are your helper. It amazes me how cruel and rude some presenters are. They get a kid to volunteer, finally, and then proceed to rip the kid apart or ask her really rude questions. "Nice outfit! I thought Halloween was later in the year." "How many channels can you get with those braces?" "Are you short for your age?" "Are you married or are you happy?" It is one thing to "kid around" with your assistants, but don't insult them.

## Never touch them "inappropriately"

Kids are taught at a very young age to be wary of strangers who try to touch them. You must safeguard yourself and be very cautious, lest an innocent gesture be misinterpreted by a child. Simply shake hands for too long and you look suspicious. Here are a few other things to avoid when you are working with volunteers: patting them on the head (or any-where else!) for a job well done; hugging them back when they rush at and hug you first; physically moving them where you need them to be instead of asking them to "stand over there". Be careful. It's unfortunate that we live in a world where parents and kids are so worried about stranger danger, but it's a reality, and you must watch yourself.

## Trust them to get it right

Give your volunteer a little time to work through a problem on his own. Many times I've seen an entertainer rip something from the hands of an assistant because the assistant needed help or was taking too long. If you must step in, ask if your volunteer would like help before you snatch it out of his

hands. Give him a chance to do as much as he can, even if he
can't do it all.

## Trouble makers

What if your volunteer turns out to be a troublemaker?
I've had kids come up on stage and immediately start acting
like jerks. They root through my stuff, roll their eyeballs,
answer questions with ridiculous responses. After years of
pondering this dilemma, I've come upon a course of action
that is so novel, so simple and so direct that I've never heard it
used by anyone else. I calmly say, point blank, but without
yelling, snarling or sneering, "Are you going to be able to
handle this, or would you rather go back to your seat so I can
pick someone else to help out?" This approach works. They
shape up or they ask to leave, it's their choice.

## Thank your volunteer

Don't pass up a chance to
reward good behavior. At the end of
her time as an assistant, recap what a
help she's been and ask for a round of
applause for her. If there's some little
gift you can give her to say "thanks",
please do it. And say the words,
"Thank You. You've been a great
assistant." in an enthusiastic tone.

*Choosing the right volunteer*
*makes the difference! It*
*makes a good show GREAT!*

# Chapter 14 • Crowd Control

Controlling the behavior of the audience is part of your job as an entertainer. What ever you do to make money by keeping kids entertained, you will have to learn how to control your audience. Here are a few things for you to keep in mind.

## Set the tone yourself

Your job is to provide an environment where each group of kids can have the best time *possible*. Take each group as far as they can go, but not over the edge. Some groups can stay in control while you push the limits of wild and crazy. Other groups are going to need you to reign in your energy. Constantly keep your finger on the "pulse" of each group you work with. Every time out their dynamics will change depending on the mix of kids in your group.

## Get the kids on your side

I don't recommend trying to be a pal or an equal with the kids. It's better to be the dynamic captain of your ship.

*When you are the captain of the ship, everyone at the show has a good time.*

Your program is a voyage. Everyone who signs on agrees that the goal of having a good time is worth mutual effort. It's important for you to trust your program is an entertaining one, truly enjoy working with kids and for you to behave the way you want the kids to behave and use the kinds of words you want them to use. Bring the kids up to your level, don't sink to theirs.

## Variety

Mixing up the activities of your program, or what you show and tell, will help to maintain the kids' interest in what you are doing. As I mentioned earlier, if they lose interest in you, they are going to start causing trouble.

## Be prepared

The better prepared you are, the less tense you will be and the more time and energy you will have to put into having fun with the kids. Simple guidelines include: Get there early. Maintain your props in working order. Anticipate problems and deal with them before they become problems. Make sure your audience is comfortable. Set up the same way every time. Practice and rehearse. Learn from your mistakes.

Parties and events are often peopled by kids who hardly know each other and are of mixed ages. Confusion kicks in when kids know different rules to the same game. And there seems to be one kid in each group who either will not play, plays too aggressively or cheats. If you're the game leader, your actions will determine whether everyone has a nice or lousy time. Some leaders make up their own games with simple rules so there will be no disputing a "call". I'm not sure if that solves problems or creates them.

## Interruptions

If in the middle of your program a pack of wild dogs streaks through the audience, that is an interruption. The kids react. They hoot and holler because they are excited, but they are not being trouble makers. A trouble maker is an individual who misbehaves in order to draw attention to himself. These hooting kids are just enjoying the diversion of those dogs.

Here's how to deal with interruptions. Remain calm. Let the kids take a look at what's going on. Have them remain seated. Recapture the kids attention. Calm them down. Tell the kids what to think about the interruption. Get another adult to deal with the interruption. (Your job is to entertain, not to police interruptions.) Redirect their energy back into your show. Ignore the interruption as best you can.

## "Freeze!"

If things are spinning out of your control, use the "Freeze!" command. Kids have heard it before, or something similar, in gym class. Once you have their attention you must issue a command or you will lose them to chaos again. Direct them immediately to sit down on their hands. It may sound crazy, but that's exactly why they will listen to you and follow your direction. Once they are seated quickly get back to the show.

## Troublemakers

Identify them early and anticipate the problems they will cause.

*Choose volunteers wisely, and they will make a big impact on your show!*

In your introduction to the group, tell the kids what you expect as far as their behavior goes. A sense of order discourages troublemakers.

Give the troublemaker a choice, "If you can't keep your hands to yourself you will have to sit with the adults." Most kids will choose to follow the rules once they realize their behavior will determine whether they stay or go.

Fights. Show personal disgust at the behavior, not the kid. It's what they did that you didn't like, not who they are. If they continue to act up they should be removed from the situation for safety reasons.

If a troublemaker breaks something on purpose or causes another kid to cry and you see it happen, stop everything immediately. Fetch the hosting adult. Calmly explain what has happened. Don't whine or moan. Remaining calm, and dealing with the problem in an open, cut and dried manner does not give the troublemaker the reward she/he is looking for.

Remember, they are only trying to get a rise out of you and the other kids. Don't let them see you get upset, just calmly deal with them.

## Adult troublemakers

They're out there. A few too many beers and they start acting up. They think they are really funny. They are not. The host adults (especially older adults in the audience) will usually shut them up. I'd suggest if you do end up with an adult troublemaker, start shooting pleading glances to individuals who might be able to help. Embarrassed spouses are the best. This has done the trick for me a number of times.

## The ultimate ultimatum

If all else has failed, and you are <u>sure</u> (from lots and lots of experience) that there's no turning this rabble of kids around and they are headed for destructive behavior, and the hosts or sponsors won't help you out even after you explain the severity of the situation to them—YOU CAN LEAVE.

You will leave without a check. You can just pack up, calmly, in silence and walk out the door. <u>Tell everyone you're sorry they couldn't control themselves, but you can see that you will be unable to do what you were hired to do</u>. Good Bye.

No one wins when it comes to this but at least you are no longer responsible for the damage that group of kids was heading toward.

## Wrap up

The success of your program lies not only in your ability to present engaging activities. Your success hinges also on your ability to read and control your audience. Entertainers tend to forget they need to build audience controls into their programs. It's not enough to present cool stuff. You must understand your audience and what motivates them. Don't wait for them to react however they will.

Use planning when creating your presentation to spark positive responses. If you do run up against a troublemaker, knowing ahead of time how to respond will keep you in control of the situation.

You can't have a program without an audience. Why and how you deal with that fact will determine your ultimate success.

# Chapter 15 • Match Age with Activity

Matching your program with kids who are likely to enjoy it is important, and an issue you need to explore whether you are working for schools or home parties. It's not wise to press activities on kids who will not be able to appreciate or handle them, no matter how much you personally enjoy the activity. A mis-match causes the kids to get bored and un-ruly, leading them into disruption!

To ensure a match, think about the age you want to work with. What interests them? How can you adapt your activities so that a particular age group will appreciate them to the utmost? As a professional children's entertainer, you don't want to get caught working for a *wrong* group of kids. With a bit of forethought you can avoid that mistake.

## Creative party planning mom nearly derailed by train experience!

While researching this book, I spoke with a mom who throws big annual shindigs for each of her three daughters. For the past ten years, she has thrown three or more parties each year. New activities and themes were prepared for each event. She loves to throw parties, and this offered her an excellent outlet for her creativity. She had birthday breakfasts, Olympic events parties, birthday at the (home) movies, rent-a-juggler shows and make your own cake parties. She was so confident in her ability to put together activities which could amuse kids for an hour or two that she volunteered to head the entertainment committee for a small club's holiday party. There, she found a challenge that was new to her.

There were 75 children at the club's party and she was struck by the difference in how the kids behaved. Here is what she told me:

*The girls spent a full hour at the craft's tables, just like I expected. The boys whipped through the crafts and wound up spending the entire party riding around and around the parking lot on a small train I'd rented as an afterthought. It's a good thing I brought that train in because those boys wanted nothing to do with any of the holiday crafts after the first five or ten minutes. I was shocked.*

In all of the years she'd been planning great parties, she'd never thrown a party for a group of boys. If boys were included in her daughter's parties, there were only one or two, usually kids from school, and they easily went along with their classmates.

Based on her experience at that one holiday party, she was worried about starting an entertainment business.

*If I had to deal often with a gang of boys, especially eight to twelve year old boys, well, I'd rather be working behind the counter at a drug store.*

She likes entertaining girls. "Girls are so *easy*", she said later. Of course they were easy for her, she had three of her own—all close in age. She was well versed in the way girls mature and what they are interested in at particular ages. She was a girl expert. She enjoyed the activities right along with the girls. Each party included eight to ten girls, all of whom were just about the same age.

My response? Specialize in girls parties. Advertise as the "expert in party fun for girls." And turn down all the other jobs. Later, with more experience, she might want to expand the range of bookings she was willing to take. Or she might find that having a well defined niche was her key to success.

## The niche works for many successful entertainers

Remember when I introduced you to the Fairy Tale Princess? She will never be invited to work with a group of nine year old boys, and that's just fine with the Princess. She wants to work for four to seven year old girls at birthday parties. No boys. No sleepovers. No mall gigs. No libraries. Just a group of five to fifteen young girls celebrating a birthday. Those are the only gigs she accepts.

I know a presenter who has a Checkers Program. He teaches seven through twelve year old kids how to play checkers. His program starts out as a presentation and finishes as a hands on activity with individual help from the Checker Man. The Checker Man put this program together because he loves the game and he wanted to teach the joys of checkers to the youngest kids he could. Six and younger are too young. He

*A program that fills an important niche—pre-teens and teens. Developing a show that reaches a specific age-range will increase your chances for success!*

really enjoys spending time with pre-teens. Once they get to be thirteen and into adulthood, he loses interest. So he focuses on 7-12 year old kids.

The Checker Man and the Princess have done a great job of mixing both their strong personal interests and an age group they can enjoy into a program that's fun to do. That's what you need to shoot for. There is no point in developing a program of activities or a theme if you are going to be stuck doing it for an age group of kids you don't enjoy. A person who loves calculus and enjoys spending time with preschoolers should plainly see a calculus program for preschoolers is a bad match.

## Do I practice what I preach?

You bet. Two of my five educational shows could easily stretch into the junior high school market. This market is desperate for quality programming. So as a test, I accepted a few bookings for seventh and eighth grade students. I discovered that I had to change the delivery and performance style of my shows too much. I really disliked doing those shows. I don't like working with thirteen and fourteen year old kids. So I stick to school kids in grade six and under; I will not accept a show that will include an audience of junior high school kids.

Remember, in this business, happiness comes from doing activities you like with kids you like. You need an age and activity match.

Here are some tips to help you think about what activities work with what kinds of kids—these are my observations from working with kids for the past ten years. Don't let these generalizations upset you. There are always exceptions to these "rules".

## <u>The difference between boys and girls</u>

Before age five and after age twelve, boys and girls are usually comfortable sharing activities, entertainments, programs and parties together. Those in between ages are the years when boys and girls activities might not mix well. This is because the kids enjoy the same activity for different reasons.

Take crafts for instance. Boys and girls both enjoy crafts activities. But, boys like to make crafts that *do things*. Girls are more likely to spend a lot of time to make a craft look great. This means that boys will get bored quickly and move on to mischief if you are expecting them to take more than 10 minutes to design and make a stained glass window. Girls can easily spend a half hour on this project. Knowing this subtle difference can mean the difference between a successful program and bedlam. If you are invited to do a party with both boys and girls, consider having extra crafts for the kids who finish early. Or design the crafts so they can be played with (for instance, everyone makes cars or rockets.) Two crafts I've seen work very successfully with both sexes are colored Sand Art (in the bottle) and spin art (paper spun on a

*Catered Children's Theme Tea Parties*

🍵 *Victorian* 🍵 *Princess*
🍵 *Ballerina* 🍵 *Bridal*

*Arts & Crafts*
*Costumes* • *Formal China*
*Arts & Crafts* • *Stories* • *Games*
*Take-Home Photos*

**One Lump or Two?**

*This is a program ~~that is generally~~ geared to girls.*

turntable as you pour paint on it). With older kids, tie-dye seems to be a big hit.

If you find that you don't like to do elaborate crafts— or to build in extras for the kids who finish quickly, then it's probably best to specialize in birthday parties for just boys or just girls. However, keep in mind that this will limit the scope of your business somewhat. Few libraries or corporate events will want to limit their audience to a single sex.

## __Age matters__

Here's an idea of what you can expect from kids, year by year.

__One and two year olds:__ Programs for this age group are usually intended as a celebration for the adults involved. The kids might be stimulated by the atmosphere but they will not understand the concept "party" or "performance". If you find yourself invited to work with this age group, the parents are really looking for a "baby sitter" not a program to keep the kids busy and entertained.

Anything you could do to involve these kids? Maybe, but it must also involve the parent in a very active way.

A parent can hold the child in their lap while you sing some fun kids songs. You could offer a play group or a "mommy and me" party. Lead the parents and kids through fun exercises that are interactive and playful for both.

__Three and four year olds:__ Movement, music and color are the keys to reaching and entertaining this age. If this is the target age for your program, you've got some work ahead of you. Parents sometimes don't understand why a professional can't keep the kids all busy and giggling for a full hour. I think a 30-40 minute maximum length program is best for these kids. (Though some four year olds with older siblings can go the hour.) And some of that time will need to be you doing presentational activities with a puppet, singing or some such.

Present simple noncompetitive games like follow the leader, do as I do, "dancing with music". You might have a ring toss area or a pots and pans parade with funny costume hats and noisy "instruments". Educational program themes might include colors, shapes, littering, simple safety and stories.

Note: Try to create good opportunities for the parents to take pictures of their little darlings. Kodak™ moments are always successful with the parents of this age group.

**Five year olds:** Think silly. This is my favorite age. Any theme can be adapted for this age, just keep it *simple*. Simple rules for games that burn a lot of energy and include opportunities to practice movements they are working on. Throwing, hitting, catching, coloring, gluing. Cooperative gamesmanship, waiting for turns, sharing of toys are learned by playing at this age. Role playing and acting games are fun. Their attention span lengthens and makes possible longer games and stories.

Have lots of prizes for this age group and many activi-

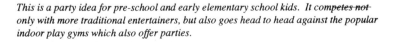

*This is a party idea for pre-school and early elementary school kids. It competes not only with more traditional entertainers, but also goes head to head against the popular indoor play gyms which also offer parties.*

ties. Try to find a way to make everyone a winner. You will win with short stories, puppet shows, music and bits of juggling.

**Six and seven year olds:** This is where you can really start getting a bit more involved and elaborate. They have more self restraint now. More natural skill that will keep them from becoming quite so frustrated. Dexterity and coordination are kicking in at this age. This means kids can be taken in with more intricate rules and levels to games and activities. They will play the old games but will not overlook violations and rule breakers like when they were younger. They like things to be organized and will take pride in competition and will strive to be the first to complete activities. Interest in crafts and arts, lifelike manipulation of puppets, hobby related activities, blossom at this age.

They will happily take part in role playing games. Let them be animals and machines. They will sit through quite a long puppet show. They can fully appreciate magic, juggling and skills.

These kids are in the first and second grade. Educational shows for them as well as the older kids that follow, can deal with any elementary school age issue. What are they learning in the classroom, science camp, after school program? They study issues such as citizenship, personal responsibility, art and history.

**Eight through twelve year olds.** Participation was invented for this age. Don't leave home without it. They are easily absorbed in whatever it is you can throw at them. That is, if you are really enthused. Don't let them think you are "talking down." Instead, pull them up to your level.

They can handle science experiments, solve mysteries, invent their own games and that's just in the first 15 minutes. There's not much you can't do with these kids. They have a high "buy in rate". They don't like clowns as much as they did when they were younger. Try not to be silly, rather be funny.

It won't take you long to figure out the difference. The only thing better than being funny is skillfully providing these kids a chance to be funny themselves.

Kids this age have fun with their own hobbies and interests, though they are always looking to acquire new ones. Teach them the joy of your hobby and share your interests. Remember, read those books about your subject that were written for this age group. Be sure to use the concepts and vocabulary that is appropriate to the age group.

Some programs I've seen go over well have been gross science programs, make-over programs and live animal/reptile programs. Feel free to share your hobby but make sure it's an engrossing subject with interesting things to see.

*Another party idea that caters to slightly older kids.*

# Chapter 16 • Managing the Technical Details of Your Program

As an entertainer you will be invited to private homes, businesses, schools and clubs. Part of being a professional kids entertainer is protecting the kids you work with, and the facility you're working in, from harm. Adapting your activities for large and small groups, poor conditions or bad weather is all part of the business. It is a good idea to go watch as many shows and programs as you can when you are just getting started. As you watch, make mental notes of how things are organized and set up. How does the entertainer or performer use the space to keep the kids focused? You will also see things that you know can be improved. Keep all of this information in mind as you develop your own show. The more information you can provide to the person who books your show, the better. We now routinely send out a one page letter which outlines everything that will make my life easier on the day of the event. This list includes asking the client to make sure the performance area has been swept! Never assume something will be taken care of. Ask!

## Technical requirements

It is your job to communicate your needs to your clients before they hire you. Can you work outside or in? If you prefer to work outside, what happens if it rains? Do you move your activities inside the school, under a tent or into the garage or will you just cancel your program? Will you need electricity to do your program? Strong lights? Access to running water? All of these things are considered technical requirements for programs. Think these things through. If you can communicate clearly, you will be able to steer clear of inappropriate bookings, and gravitate toward venues to which your act is well suited!

## Steer clients to the best space possible

When a potential client calls to book your program, you have your first and best opportunity to avoid a lot of confusion later on. Ask about the space where the show will be held. Be up front about your needs. Do you need a certain ceiling height? Table space? Draft free area? Well ventilated area? Easy access to outside? Room on the floor for all of the kids to sit? A sink nearby? A room that is already kid proofed? By communicating your technical needs when you are talking to a potential client, and asking if they will be able to provide you with these needs, you will avert problems. If the client agrees to host your program, they will have an accurate picture of what it is you will be doing and what you will need to have on the day of the event. They can make their booking decision based on all of the facts.

Once you have the show booked, it is a good idea to confirm any special needs with the sponsor in writing.

*This is our standard contract. Parties and other smaller programs may not need such a formal agreement; a letter of confirmation may suffice.*


How do you prepare your list of technical requirements? Ask yourself these questions. What do you need to do to protect the contents of the room from harm? Will tables need to be moved? Will you need tables to set your stuff up on? Do you need a sound system? A draft free space? Will you be bringing a drop cloth on the floor? Will you need more light? Do you need a wall where you can hang games or crafts?

## Ground rules for the kids & safety

To ensure the safety of your audience, you need to control yourself and encourage the kids to stay under control. Whatever rules you expect the kids to follow, make sure they hear and comprehend them up-front at the beginning of your program. And follow the rules yourself. Set a good example.

While you are setting up your show, ask about the location of key places, so that during a show, you can point out where the bathroom is, where the boundaries are, where they can get a drink, and so forth. If there are "house rules" at a private event, find out from the host just what they are, and tell the kids up front.

Also tell them that you're all going to have lots of fun but there are a few ground rules—just like in physical education (gym class) in school. They might include: Have fun and play hard, play safe, play fair and no swearing. If you have a question about what you should be doing, ask me. That's why I'm here. There is to be no screaming. No running. Keep your hands to yourself. If you need to go to the bathroom, tell an adult. No snacking during the activity time.

If you are performing outdoors, try set up in the shade. Kids can get over heated fast. They have little taste for moderation and they will keep on running around until they break down due to heat exhaustion. Also, the sun can be a killer. Its bright light strains eyes, causes headaches, burns skin, superheats playground equipment and blacktop. Know where the sun is and whenever possible, get those kids into shade.

Before you get the kids running around, check for trouble. Are there sticks, holes in the ground, dog doo, low hanging branches, bee hives, loose cats, busy streets, pricker bushes, flower beds, stone walls, mud pits... If there are these sorts of things around, warn the kids. Don't trust them to use their common sense to avoid a problem. Move what you can.

Place landmarks as reminders. Set boundaries. Remember: If you aren't prepared, anything that can go wrong will likely go wrong—at the worst possible moment.

## Be prepared to adapt

You will want to have some back up activities ready to go if your planned activities will not work in the space provided by the sponsor.

Don't try to force your activities into a space that will not accept them. The last thing you want to do is stain the carpets because the table is too small, or put holes in the ceiling because it's too low for a safe game of smash the pinata, or break a collectable plate with an indoor game of dodge-ball.

## Coping with the weather

If you have an outdoor program that can not be brought indoors (with some planned modification) you are going to be in trouble. As you create your program, keep asking yourself, "Okay, what if right now the sky opened up and it started pouring?" Or, "What if it was one of those days where the wind is so loud I won't be able to be heard? What would I do?"

Parents who plan for an outdoor party/event are not easily swayed by dark clouds, monsoon winds or drizzle. More often than not, you will be told to, "... give it a try outside first. When it starts raining we'll figure out what to do."

Know that at some point or another, everything you use in your program will be rained on. It might blow away. Take that into account in your program planning stage.

## Dealing with distractions

Buzzing bees, airplanes, trash trucks, kids across the street, the television blaring in the next room, or a crowd of adults chattering in the back of the room. You will be fighting to keep the kid's attention. It's amazing how a single thing or event can lure those kids so soundly away from your control. And it happens fast!

You will be standing there readying them for a kick-ball game and unbeknownst to you, the pony wagon pulls into the driveway! The kids are off like a shot and you are left with mud in your face.

Plan where you want the kids to be facing as they watch and listen to you. Make it easy for them to see you and only you. Put your back to as flat and plain a background as possible. That may be the side of a garage or against a hedge row. Have those kids look into the direction less likely to produce a distraction. Try to be the only interesting thing they can see.

**The moral of this chapter is simple: You've got to anticipate problems if you hope to avoid them.**

# Chapter 17 • Fees, Profits and Expenses

When I suggest to people that they should consider making money by entertaining kids, the most common response is, "I don't know what I would do or how much I would charge". We spent the first part of this book exploring ways to make money by keeping kids busy and entertained. Let's take a few pages now to help you figure out whether all the effort would be worth it.

Let's tackle these questions: Based on your hometown and surrounding area, how much can you charge for the kind of program you're thinking of doing? And, how much of that fee will be profit?

There's a lot that goes into determining fees. I've included enough information here to demystify the process for you a bit. It's as much as you need to get you started. Setting fees is a pretty tricky business. For a more detailed discussion of this issue, you might want to read our detailed special report called *Setting Fees*.

# Determine the fee range for your market

How do you do this? Ask your competition. They may not tell you exactly what they charge but they should give you the range in your area for shows like theirs. Ask the folks who you would like to work for. What do they expect to pay for an entertainer who provides your kind of service? Ask how much they paid for their last program, what the presenter did and whether they were happy. Get out to see your competitor's programs and see for yourself what customers expect from the presenters. How does what you do compare to what they do? Determining the fee range is an important step in setting your price, though it's not the only factor.

## The fee equation

The basic equation for setting fees is as follows:

Cost of your materials + operating expenses + the value you place on your time and expertise = fee. Let's take a look at each part of the equation.

## Cost of your materials

The materials that you use in each program are part of your fee. In my family variety show, JUST FOR THE FUN OF IT, I do a little juggling, a couple of simple magic tricks and a few balloon animals. I have to pay for my balloons, expendable magic supplies (such as giveaway HAT TEARS and the rope that gets cut up every show). My juggling props are reusable, but still need to be replaced or repaired from time to time — expenses which need to be paid for. When I total this up, it costs me about $5.00 in materials each time I perform this show.

## Operating expenses

Also called <u>overhead</u>. These are the expenses that keep your business running. These fall into different categories.

<u>Advertising</u>: The cost of printing cards, fliers, bro-

chures, taking out ads etc.

Telephone and utilities: If you are working from home, you need to include the amount of your phone bill that reflects business usage, plus the percentage of utilities (heat, electric, etc.) your business activities consume.

Maintenance of equipment, vehicles or workspace: How many business miles are you going to drive? Are you planning to use a computer for business purposes? You need to recoup the business use of these things. It may not seem like much but it can add up. In 1997, the IRS allows $.31 per business mile to cover gas, and maintenance for your business vehicle. That's nearly $1.25 for a booking that's 2 miles from your home (you'd put four miles on your car, round-trip).

Stationery and office supplies: You will need to buy envelopes, paper, pens. Everything that's useful, and exclusively used for your business, needs to be accounted for in your fee. Again, these little things are potentially a small amount until you add them together.

Accounting, legal and other professional services: If you decide that you need to talk to other working professionals (accountants, lawyers) with questions about helping you run your business, their fees are part of your overhead.

Business related dues, subscriptions and classes: My membership in The International Jugglers Association, my subscription to *Laughmakers Magazine*, my balloon bending how-to books, all of these things are part of my overhead.

Overhead expenses add up. Make sure to build them into your fee. Add up what you need to get started (and I suggest you economize as much as possible on everything except advertising!) then divide by the number of shows you think you can do this year. That number is the cost you should apply to each show for "overhead". Failure to do the math may mean that your business fails to make a profit!

## The value you place on your time and expertise

You can choose to donate your services if you like.

My guess is that you would rather earn some money to compensate you for the time it took to create your program and the effort it took to deliver it. You have to set a value on your time and effort, and many people have a tough time doing that.

## To make it all a little easier, try this. . .

After adding together your cost of overhead and materials, how much more will it take to bring you up to the *mid point* in the fee range you determined earlier? The difference between your actual cost and the price range mid point is how much your time and effort are worth.

Example: The range for shows like yours is $75-$125. Mid Point is $100. The total cost for your materials and overhead works out to be $30. per show. That means your time and effort are worth $70. per show. Do you feel $70. per show compensates you fairly for your time and effort? If so, go for it! If not, at least you can cut your losses early and try to put together a program that would give you a greater profit return per show. Or, try to get your program into a better paying market.

## Different prices for different markets

While we're talking about fees, here's another interesting point you should think about.

My birthday presentation fee is $125 for 55 minutes of work within a half hour from my house. That includes a show and then balloons for up to 20 kids. But at a preschool, that same show without balloons for the kids runs 40 minutes and costs $225. At a mall I'll do that show for $350, and sometimes they only want a half hour. How do I get away with charging different amounts for the "same show"? It's all about "markets". Different markets have different fees because I'm filling different needs.

At a birthday, there are only a few kids. The fee range is lower than in other markets because this kind of program requires less skill and expertise which means there are a greater number of performers who can do the job.

A mid week preschool show will have up to 75 kids. More skill is required to keep this larger group entertained. And, there are fewer presenters available to do shows during the day, mid week.

A mall will have up to 400 people at a show. They need an entertainer who is highly skilled, well known (thus able to attract people to the mall to eat and shop), and will reflect the quality the mall itself tries to reflect in the community. Malls might also require a sound system and they certainly want glossy photos and a sample press release from me to use in their publicity. Not to mention the one or two million dollars worth of liability insurance I must have. They demand a lot, there are not many performers who can fill the bill, so the fee range starts much higher. That's why I can charge so much more for a mall than for a birthday.

## <u>Wrap up</u>

I hope all this discussion of prices, expenses, fees and everything else has helped demystify this part of the business for you. Don't put off the fun that comes from entertaining kids just because you don't know how much you should charge. That's ridiculous!

These are the kinds of questions you should be asking and answering for yourself, *before* you get too far along in the process of creating your program. Are those potential customers that you have in mind going to be interested in your program? How much are they going to be willing to pay you for it? Based on projected expenses, will you be able to earn enough to be happy? I once spent eight months creating a forty five minute show only to realize (too late) no one would be interested in buying it. Oops!

# Part 3 • The Business of Show Business

# Chapter 18 • Advertising for Entertainers

So, how are you going to spread the word about your new show or entertainment service? How are those potential customers going to know to call *you* when they need an entertainer? It all starts with you.

## Word of mouth

Word of mouth starts with your mouth. You should tell all your friends about this new little business of yours. Ask them to call if they hear about any jobs or if they are shopping for an entertainer for themselves or an event they are helping to put together. You can also take your word of mouth directly to potential customers.

## Use the phone as a business tool

When I was starting out, I spent a lot of time going

*This yellow page ad generated tons of work, but I still didn't sit around and wait for the phone to ring. Even after ten years in business, I use a combination of the marketing tools mentioned in this chapter to keep the phones ringing and the calendar full.*

through the yellow pages. I called party planners, caterers, entertainment agencies and bureaus, special event planners, party supply stores, restaurants that host kid's birthdays, children's librarians, nursing homes, shopping center and mall offices. I called everyone I could think of who might have a group of kids who needed to be entertained for an hour or so. The goal of my call was simple, to let them know that I could provide entertaining activities for kids, and would they like more information? It worked. I got work, fast. Why not let *your* fingers do the walking?

## Business cards

Cheap and effective, these little slips of paper go a long way. They make it easier for folks to remember you and your number (especially if you are not in the yellow pages), you can tack them on public bulletin boards and leave stacks behind with whomever you are working for. They even make great goody bag stuffers.

Don't treat them like precious works of art. They will do you no good sitting in your desk drawer at home. Make a game out of giving away five of your business cards every day. Include them in your correspondence. Hand them out liberally.

## Repeat business

It's easier to keep a happy customer than it is to win a

*Even simple announcements, like this one, generate good publicity for events.*

new one.

Why then do so many entertainers neglect their past customers? That list of past jobs is a gold mine to be tapped every year. Contact them a couple of months ahead of their event and ask if they would like to have you back again.

Churches will have summer socials every year. Preschools will always have holiday parties. Kids who have birthday parties at the age of four will likely have a few more by the time they are ten or eleven. Schools all plan to present three to eight programs every year. Repeat business should be a healthy percentage of your work.

## Donated shows for exposure

It won't take long before you get these offers. They will promise, in exchange for your services, that you will get lots of free publicity, all the food you can eat and an almost certain shot at getting your mug on the evening news. What should you do? It's up to you, but there are some things you should know.

You will get lots of these offers so you can feel free to be selective. Choose those that promise a good return or those that you believe offer a valuable community service. Keep in mind that your chances of getting free publicity are slim to none. If you take a lot of these, you *will* become known as the entertainer who works for free. And lastly, if everyone else — the caterer, moon-bounce people, face painters and tent rental people — is getting paid, you should be paid too. If everyone concerned is donating their time and efforts, the chances are good that this event is worthy of your consideration.

## An answering machine

Clients expect to play phone tag — they don't expect to hear the phone ring without any answer at all. Get a machine. Record an informative message on it. Return calls promptly.

## Newspaper articles and photos

This is the easiest way to get thousands of dollars of free publicity. The fact that you can keep kids entertained and busy will mean that at some point you will be doing "public" events. Public events attract the press. The press looks to include community activities, kids, school happenings, local happenings in their papers. It happens to me dozens of times a year. For instance, I recently did a show for a school in Connecticut. They sent a press release out to their local small town paper saying that I was coming to their school. The reporter came in, asked a few questions, watched the show and took a few photos. Tomorrow it will be a local interest story. Next week, the school will send me a clip of the article and I will copy it to use to sell future shows. Meanwhile, that picture or little article inspires the local scout master to ask the school principal for my phone number because they have a blue and gold banquet coming up and they need a program.

May the press be with you.

# Brochures

In a standard two fold, three panel, front and back brochure, here's what you will want to include: At least two nice photos. Quotes from happy customers. A description of your offerings, written so the client will see the advantages of hiring you rather than just a description of your show. A small biography. Contact information. And, the whole piece should reflect your character and style.

# Fliers

These are usually single sheet, single sided 8.5 X 11 pieces of colored stock paper. Since there's less room for you to promote yourself, all the information must be shortened and simplified. A photo is a must. Contact information, quotes, a brief show description written with a specific client type in mind should be enough.

Sometimes these are printed on glossy paper to look like little posters and when they are, they make nice pieces to autograph—post show. That way your photo will end up hanging on the kid's bedroom wall or maybe even on the fridge where your name and number will

*"Excellent"*
— Janet Campbell, Mansfield, MA

Look to Keith M. Johnson for a party which offers—

• 50 minutes of pure entertainment

• Juggling, Magic and Balloon Creatures

• Shows the Kids and Adults will Enjoy!

**Fees Start at $95!**

*Call Keith M. Johnson for more details*
23 Wildwood Avenue, Providence RI 02907 • Phone / Fax (401) 781-6676 or (800) 730-6676 • E-Mail KMJH@aol.com

—COUPON—

*Mention this coupon when you book a birthday party or holiday event and receive $5 off our regular prices!*
*CALL TODAY! (401) 781-6676 or, outside Providence, (800) 730-6676*

*This is the flyer I designed in 1993 to hand out during a summer tour of 35 Rhode Island libraries. I included a coupon so that I could track the returns.*

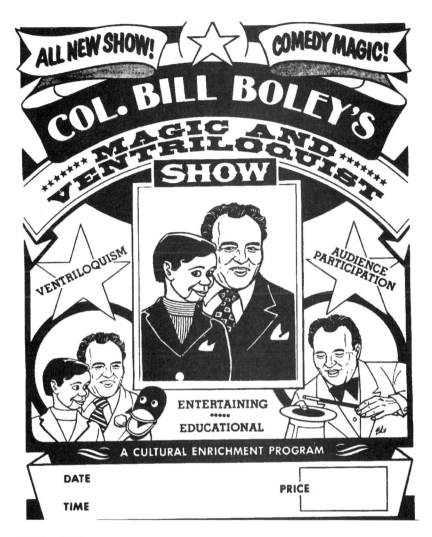

*This flier doubles as a poster.*

always be there to remind the parents how to get hold of you for their next party or function.

## Letters

It's been said that George Bush got elected President because his wife Barbara kept a massive Christmas card list, and she kept in touch with all of those "friends" they'd met over the years who could be counted on to support George. Do you have a holiday card list? Do your parents if they live in your community? Networking with letters can be a very effective means of launching a small business.

If you want to branch out from people who already know you, try calling a list broker (listed in the yellow pages under "mailing lists"). They can sell you lists of just about everything imagineable. We have purchased lists of corporations in our area, schools, libraries, and shops. You can even buy lists of families in certain areas of your state or city that earn a certain amount, have a credit card, have kids, and subscribe to specific magazines. Creating a postcard or letter to mail to these folks, to let them know you are available may be a good idea.

The computer now offers many opportunities for compiling lists. We have a handy little CD-ROM called SELECTPHONE which lets us compile mailing lists of businesses and individuals by zip code and neighborhood, anywhere in the country. Similar programs are offered for free on the internet.

The key to advertising your new business is to keep track of responses and costs. If an ad, letter, or method makes money—it's cheap, no matter what it costs. If it doesn't bring in any new clients, it cost too much, even if it was free.

# Chapter 19 • Agents

There are really two ways to get a job as an entertainer. One is to use the methods described in the last chapter to reach individual clients. The other is to work with an agent. Working with an agent can be fairly profitable in the beginning, but in most cases, work from an agent will only supplement the work you are finding on your own. What is an agent, and how do you find one?

An agent represents a number of entertainers. Some specialize just in school shows, other in birthday parties and family events. Others will book everything from singing telegrams to balloon deliveries to strippers.

The benefits of working for an agent are numerous. When you work with an agent, or party planner, a caterer, or an entertainment bureau, as they are all pretty much the same thing, you sell them *once* on the strength of your show and if they think they can make money working with you, they will work with you. From then on a piece of their advertising expenses, office staff expenses, reputation and market position

*An example of an agent's ad. You will find these in the yellow pages, in family oriented newspapers, and magazines. Give them a call and see if they'll work with someone with your skills*

goes to promote you and other members of their stable.

If you can find an agent you can trust to pay you on time and sell your program with integrity, they are worth what ever they can get, on top of your going rate. That's especially true in the beginning of your career when you don't have too much money to invest in advertising or too much time on the phone doing cold calls. Agents will have you working venues that would have taken you years to break into on your own. The experience you get from this kick-in-the-pants start to your career will prepare you to be successfully independent in time. That's if you ever want to break away. Some performers rely on their agents for their entire careers. I wouldn't have been happy letting someone else control my destiny in that way, but a number of performers I know are happy to turn over a cut of their income in exchange for not having to worry about "the business" of performing.

You see, I always considered agent generated bookings gravy. I never counted on them for my survival. In this area, at least, there are few agents who can keep you busy full time, and I've chosen to make performing my full-time business since 1986. In order to pay the bills and earn a living, I felt I had to go out on my own. Sure, I was happy to take a booking from an agent if I had the day free and the money was right. But I was never comfortable waiting around for them to call.

In fact, as my reputation grew, and the success of my own promotional efforts mounted, I was able to wean myself from agent generated business altogether. My name and show were well enough known and my advertising was so fine tuned that I was popular enough to book shows on my own at major events, parties and shows, without the added cache of an agent to get my foot in the door.

How can you get yourself hooked up with an agent? Contact them and offer to stop by and meet them face to face. Be prepared with a quick demonstration of your skills if they want it. There are very few agents who will "sign you" to an exclusive contract. That kind of agent is a scarce commodity, and most of them are not taking on new clients. The agents you will be working with will represent a bunch of entertainers who can do birthdays, picnics, strolling entertainment and smaller festivals. They will give you a try. If you do a good job, show up on time, then ask the client to mention to your agent how much they liked your show. Since you can only pass out the agent's business cards at their bookings, these kind words will increase your chances of getting more work from that particular agent. You want your name to be fresh in the agent's mind when he is fielding calls so thank him regularly and keep him up to date as far as the skills you offer in your shows and any new venues you'd like to work.

Know too that since the agent doesn't sign you "exclusively" you can be listed with a number of agents at the same time in the same area. Check the yellow pages for entertainment agencies, independent party planners and balloon delivery services. Call them all and offer to meet with them. They will be happy to hear from you because they are always on the lookout for fresh faces and acts. But, be wary of them before you know them. Some agents are fly-by-nights and they will play games with your paycheck or with your schedule. Some will send you into jobs where you are totally out of place. Check their references as carefully as they will check yours before you sign on the bottom line.

# Chapter 20 • Keeping Good Records

Another fear of neophyte business owners is the book-keeping. But don't let this stand in the way of having a success-ful business. It's not as hard as you may think. After you set up a simple system, you can spend as little as a fifteen minutes a day updating your business records and everything will be orderly. You may even reduce your tax bill, and most impor-tantly, you'll have the ammunition to survive an audit. Accord-ing to CONSUMER REPORTS, small business owners, espe-cially those who receive a significant amount of income in cash and report a net profit of under $100,000. a year, can expect especially close scrutiny if the IRS man comes to call. Why? Because unreported cash income, the so-called underground economy, drains billions of dollars from the IRS's coffers each year. And during an audit, the burden of proof is on you, the taxpayer. The IRS wins over 80% of all audits, mostly because the average taxpayer keeps lousy records!

Worried? Don't panic yet. Statistically, only 2.5 of

every 100 small business owners will be audited this year. However, if that shoe box is overflowing, and you're not sure where your receipts and contracts are for this week, let alone last month, it's time to take action. Here are ten tips for making bookkeeping easy, and audit proof.

## Are you a hobby or a business?

Unless you work consistently, and have no other source of income, be prepared to explain why you consider yourself a business rather than a hobby. If the IRS decides you're trying to write off the expenses of your hobby by calling it a business, you'll only be allowed to write off expenses to the amount of income you earn. How can you show that your mini-business is trying to earn a profit? Keep clear accurate financial records, and a booking calendar. Prove that you're actively looking for work as a juggler by keeping a file of news clippings, advertisements, reviews, brochures, and business cards. If the IRS is convinced you're trying to make a go of it professionally, they are less likely to stick you with the hobbyist label, even if you operated at a loss.

## Keep your records simple, but make sure you keep them!

Establish a clear paper trail of your income and expenses. If you're maintaining inventory and selling something—such as videos of your act or T-shirts, you'll need professional advice from a tax consultant or CPA. But, if the only income you earn is from your shows, it's fairly easy to set up a system which will allow you to respond quickly to an auditor's inquiries. Keep your calendar up to date, and keep a written contract for every show. The contract should outline the fee, the time and date of the performance and any other contractual obligations, such as an agreement to reimburse travel and hotel expenses. Contracts should be signed by you (or your representative) and the person hiring you. When payment is received, write the check number and date on the contract. If a reimbursement check for expenses is received later, that check number and amount should be noted, too. A photo copy of all checks is helpful, but hand written records are acceptable, especially if they correspond to bank deposits. Resist the urge to cash a check, even when you urgently need the money. Depositing all checks reflects favorably on you during an audit, because it indicates you are trying to establish a clean paper trail.

## Don't try to beat the system by stashing your cash

Cash income deserves special attention. If you often work for tips, or receive your payment in cash, the law requires you to make a daily record. Whether you use your booking calendar or a separate log really doesn't matter, as long as you're writing the numbers down. Tax fraud is a serious offense; if you are found guilty of intentionally under-reporting your income, you are responsible for paying the back taxes, plus interest, plus a fraud penalty of 75 percent of what you failed to pay. You may even end up with a criminal record.

## The best way to reduce your tax bill is to keep good records

Keep track of your expenses! Most small business owners lose hundreds, if not thousands of dollars a year, because they're sloppy about the little expenses. Keep your receipts, and make notes on them as you make the purchase. Even if your idea of record keeping is shoveling everything into a shoe box and letting your accountant figure it out, taking 10 seconds to make those notes at the time of purchase will save you from trying to piece together each purchase on April 14. A journal is accepted as a written record of purchases under $25. Personally, I've always found it confusing to keep some receipts and throw others away. So we've gotten in the habit of writing on, and keeping, all of our receipts. At the end of this chapter, I've listed a number of frequently overlooked expenses.

## Keep it short & simple

Set up a simple system, and use it consistently. The IRS doesn't require you use any particular format, as long as the records clearly reflect your income and expenses. Most of us hate bookkeeping, and would rather be rehearsing, working or reading. However, it is as important, and necessary, as any of those activities. The key is to organize your files in a way which makes sense to you. Many performers label a series of file folders with the categories the IRS suggests for entertainers (See the end of this chapter for a list.) We've found this system contrary to how we work; at our house, as we tend to gang purchases on one receipt for several categories. It developed into little piles labeled "needs to be photocopied". Our system organizes our income and expenses by month. Travel receipts, for hotels, tolls, etc. are stapled to the contract to which they apply. When the check comes in, we note the number and date of deposit on the contract. These are all kept in an accordion file. Receipts for expenses which don't apply to a single show are kept in the same place. To keep them under control, we attach individual credit card receipts to the bill. Receipts for cash and check purchases are kept in a #10 envelope within the file, and each receipt is labeled with the store name, amount, and item. Our system isn't fancy, but with the help of our computer, we're able to find the backup paperwork for every source of income and expense in a matter of minutes.

## Carefully document odd deductions

Document expenses or deductions which may seem odd to an auditor. If you perform with items which could have been purchased for personal use—I now juggle toilet paper in one of my shows, for instance—take a photo of the prop in action. This proves that you aren't trying to write off personal expenses. If you're taking a big write off for something—you recently hired a consultant to develop a new show, for example—you might want to add a note explaining this when you file your 1040. Explaining a greatly increased deduction in advance may stave off an audit all together.

## Become a logger

The IRS recognizes that most computers, video cameras and cars are not used just for business and they are on the look out for people who bury personal expenses in their business. If you enter an audit unable to justify the percentage of business use you've written off, the deduction may be denied. Keep a log recording all business use of equipment including computers, cellular phones, video cameras, and cars.

## Eat it and reap

According to 1997 tax law, you can deduct 50% of the cost of meals eaten while away from home overnight on business. One way to avoid the extra paperwork (and save money!) is to ask your clients to reimburse you directly for your expenses on the road. Another is to take advantage of the IRS's standard meal allowance. Instead of keeping actual receipts for business meals eaten on the road, you to claim from  $26 to $38 a day, depending on where you traveled. IRS publication 463 lists the per diem amount allowed for most major cities. It is perfectly legal to claim $38 a day for food in New York City, even if you only ate two bagels. (You will, however, only be able to deduct $19 a day—the 50% limitation applies.) A 50% deduction for business meals is allowed, too, as long as you document who attended and the purpose of the meeting. You are still allowed to deduct 100% of your accommodation expenses, even if your spouse or companion travels with you. Just be prepared to prove that you were actually working in Aruba or Honolulu!

## Bring in the subs

Do you hire other entertainers to perform at events with or for you? The government is keen on finding employers who call their employees subcontractors to avoid paying taxes and benefits. Ask each of your performers to sign a letter outlining the terms of your relationship; this will document the fact that everyone knew what was going on. It helps to work only with subs who either book shows on their own, or who rely on someone other than you for work. Keep records which show that your subcontractors, are, in fact, self-employed people who are actively pursuing their own business interests. For more information on the differences between employees and subcontractors, read **The IRS, Independent Contractors, and You** by James Urquhart (Fidelity Publishing Co.).

## Home office, fact or fiction?

Taking a write off for a portion of your rent or mortgage through the home office deduction remains a sticky issue. Before taking the home office deduction, consult a tax professional. Recent court rulings have taken a limited view of who qualifies. If you store inventory in your home, you may be able to take a deduction for that space; otherwise, be prepared to prove that you meet these three requirements: A. that the space is used regularly and exclusively for business, B. that it is the principle place in which you do business, and C. that it be a separately identifiable space in your home. Keep in mind, though, that your business expenses (including a portion of your electricity and other utilities bills) are deductible no matter where they occurred, and whether or not you take the home office deduction.

In conclusion, keeping accurate records does require some time, but it need not take over your life. Think through a system which makes sense to you, then spend a little time each day updating your records and receipts. At tax time (and at audit time) you'll be able to breathe easy with the knowledge that you can back up your return.

## Frequently overlooked deductions

According to Fred Daily, an expert tax attorney and the author of TAX SAVVY FOR SMALL BUSINESSES (NOLO PRESS), these are some of the most frequently overlooked business expenses

Promotional expenses
bank service charges
business gifts
business related books and magazines
casualty and theft losses
charitable contributions
commissions
consultant fees
credit bureau fees
interest on credit cards for business purchases
interest on personal loans used for business purposes
office supplies
on-line computer services related to business
parking, meters, tolls
petty cash funds
postage
seminars and conventions
taxi or bus fare
telephone calls when you're away from home on business

## IRS suggested categories for entertainers

Agents' Commissions: Invoices from agents who book you.

Advertising: Invoices for ads placed in the yellow pages, newspapers, magazines, etc.

Continuing Education: receipts for conventions, workshops, and lessons. (Note, the classes must be directly related to your current career or one to which you aspire. A Learning Annex course on meeting your soul mate wouldn't be deductible)

Cosmetics: Theatrical makeup.

Costumes: Store receipts for special clothes which are worn exclusively at performances. Also includes dry cleaning receipts.

Entertainment: Receipts for diners at which you entertained subcontractors, clients and other jugglers. Each receipt should detail who was present, and the purpose of the meeting.

Fees/Dues/Subscriptions: Receipts for professional organization dues, and business related magazines.

Health Care: If your doctor bills, prescriptions, or doctor mandated special equipment exceeds a certain percentage of your income, it is deductible. Don't forget to record the mileage of driving to and from the doctor's office or hospital. It counts toward your total, too.

Insurance: Business liability insurance, auto insurance, and health insurance.

Lodging: Receipts for hotel bills. If your client is paying, you'll have to show the IRS that the expenses offset the amount you claimed for reimbursements.

Office Supplies: Receipts for business related computer equipment, paper clips, envelopes, letterhead, etc.

Parking/Tolls/Cabs: These receipts really add up. You'll be surprised.

Professional Services: Advise from lawyers, accountants, consultants, etc.

Postage Delivery: Bills for UPS, messenger services, and the Post Office.

Promotion: Invoice for printing, brochure designers, photo processors, video tape dubbing, etc.

Prop Supplies: Receipts from dealers or any store from whom you bought props.

Telephone: Business related phone bills. If you only have one line, you can't write off the basic service. You are allowed to write off any business related long distance calls or special services.

Travel: Airline Tickets and Car Rental Receipts.

Utilities: Gas, electric, and water bills. You may be able to deduct a small portion of these if your office or studio is in your home.

# Chapter 21 • Working from Home

Whether you want to entertain kids full-time or part-time, chances are you will run your business from your home, at least in the beginning. Here are some tips to help keep you organized and motivated at home.

## Be prepared

You're reading this book, and that's a good start. But before you go into business, you'll need to check to see if you'll need special insurance or licenses for your new business. For instance, most malls and many daycare centers require that entertainers provide them with a certificate that confirms that they carry $1 million dollars of business liability insurance.

Even something as simple as your business name will have to be approved. If you use your full name as your business name—such as "Judy's Smith's Tea Parties" you may not need to register a ficticious business name. However, if you operate your business as "Tea Parties for Tots" you will undoubtedly need a special license (sometimes call a DBA or Ficitious Name Statement that links your name to your business name. One way to register a name is to incorporate, then the secretary of state in your state will perform a search to make sure the name you've chosen is original and not in use by someone else. If you are not planning to incorporate, call your city or town hall and ask how to register a business name. They should be able to point you in the right direction.

To make the red tape of a business start up less threatening, many states now have a business center which will lead you through the process of applying for the proper licenses and registrations. Check with your the secretary of state's office, or consult the local library, city hall or county seat to ask about specific laws in your state.

## Create a workspace

Sure, you'll be spending most of your actual work hours at other venues—other people's homes for parties, or the local school—but you'll probably still need a space at home where you can keep the phone and your files. (This may or may not qualify you for an IRS home-office deduction. Consult the IRS, a tax attorney, CPA, or enrolled agent to review your unique circumstances.)

Most experts advise putting your office in a separate room, such as a spare bedroom or in the basement. When our office was upstairs in the spare bedroom of our big drafty house, we dreaded going to work because the office was too hot or too cold. Our office is now on the first floor of the house—in the front room of a large double parlor. We moved our television and sofa up to that spare bedroom, making it our "living room". Now it's usually too hot or too cold to watch TV, which makes us more productive! The moral of this story is to put your office where-ever you are likely to work. Don't feel obligated to put it in a spare room just because the "experts" say so.

Whatever room you choose, make the necessary changes to ensure that this space is clearly and exclusively used for business. It is a hassle to clear the "office" off the kitchen table at dinner time. Or to re-type a contract because your kid spilled juice on it. Clearly outlines the boundaries of your new office if you want the kids to keep their sticky hands off your stuff.

## Do you need a computer?

It will make your life much easier, but it's not essential. If all you need it for is to design flyers and brochures, it may be cheaper to have the designer at the copy-print place put it together for you. Or you can design the "old fashioned" way, using a typewriter to set the type, and then pasting up your original copies with rubber cement. That's what I did in the beginning!

Computerized record keeping will make life easier, but it's not essential. My brother in law runs a successful one-man law firm, and he insists on balancing the books by hand. As I've mentioned before, we have found that computerization helped us get organized and stay that way. A personal finance program, such as Quicken or Microsoft Money comes pre-programmed on many new computers, or can be purchased for around $50. Unless you sell merchandise and maintain inventory, these simple program will be sufficient. (More elaborate accounting systems, such as PEACHTREE or QUICKBOOKS, are currently available for under $150.) Personally, we use QUICKEN. We are able to categorize every item we enter, so we're confident that our records clearly reflect our business income and expenses. All we have to do is enter our income and expenses and the computer will figure how much we've spent on props, where our income is coming from, and our net worth. It also spares me the headaches associated with chasing down the pennies that throw manual systems out of balance. To boot, most systems are compatible with the tax preparation software; download your files, and your tax returns are about 80% complete!

Perhaps the best use of a computer is to maintain customer lists. It makes it easy to print labels and do mailings. But it's not a necessity. When Mary was working as a fund-raiser, they kept all of their donor records on index cards . . . and they raised $1 million a year. Sometimes keeping your records as simple as possible is best. It leaves you more time to focus on the important priorities in your business.

## The business phone

In the family entertainment business, most customers understand that you are a small business operating out of your home. Therefore, they accept little inconveniences like answering machines. However, you will lose jobs if your phone is answered unprofessionally, or if your answering machine message is so generic that your customers think they've dialled the wrong place. Here's what I recommend. If you are only going to have one phone line in your house, make it a business line (if you ask the phone company to convert your current line into a business line, the costs will be significantly cheaper than if you have a new "business" line installed in your home). The advantage of the business line is that it entitles you to advertise in the yellow pages. Most of the entry level work in this business—such as birthday parties and family events—is booked by people who start their search in the yellow pages.

Now that you have a business line, consider a distinctive ring service. This costs under $10 a month, and for it, the phone company gives you a second number that will ring through on your phone line. Each number has a different ring. This service is much cheaper than running two lines into the house, and it is a necessity if you have children in the home. They can be taught which ring they may answer, and which they should let you (or the answering machine) pick up. Trust me, the fastest way to look like a rank amateur is to have your youngster answer the phone and bawl, "whatdja want?". Until your kids are old enough to answer the phone in a business like manner, and to take accurate messages, they should not answer your business phone. This is a competitive business. As I said earlier, your customers understand you are working from home, but they will not be forgiving if they cannot leave a message because a toddler answered the phone, or if their call is not returned within 24 hours because your teen "forgot" to give you the message. The work will go to the folks who make the effort to be professional, no matter where they keep their workspace!

To assist you in being professional, buy a good quality answering machine. It needn't be fancy, but it should not make your voice sound as if you recorded the message under water. Record an informational, business like outgoing message. Think of your answering machine as a mini-brochure, working for you when you cannot make it to the phone. Avoid messages such as "you've reached 555-1212, please leave a message." These types of messages make the customer wonder if she has copied the number correctly. For years, we only had one phone line, which had business message on it. Our friends and family knew they could reach us at that number. And they knew that we don't like to take personal calls during the day, as that tied up the phone.

Many phone companies now offer a voice mail system that eliminates the need for an answering machine. The biggest advantage to voice mail is that voice mail will pick up when you are on the phone with another client. (If you use an answering machine, the second caller will get a busy signal.) It adds an additional monthly expense, but you may find that it is worth it, especially if you have kids who talk on the phone for hours during the day!

# Chapter 22 • Managing Your Kids and Maintaining Your Life

Many of us choose to work from home so that we can reduce or eliminate day care expenses. Or so that we can be active participants in our children's lives. These are both admirable goals, but know at the outset that working from home isn't always easy. It may require your family to make sacrifices and hard decisions.

Sit down with your family before you start your business. Let them know if there are new ground-rules, such as limits on phone calls, their need to be more self-reliant so you can work on weekends, the need to cut the budget in other places so that you have capital to run your business with until you develop a client base, and so forth. Keeping the lines of communication open will make life easier for everyone.

# The childcare issue

It is possible to juggle home and family. And it's much easier to do so when your house is the home base for your work. I've read stacks of interviews with parents who work from home, and many of them say that day-care is essential. I don't agree, and would argue that many of the parents I talk to list raising their own kids as a key reason why they started a home based business. Everyone's situation is different, and you may find that you need the help of a baby-sitter or daycare center. However, we have managed quite nicely without outside help.

When we started our family, my wife, Mary, quit her job to work with me full-time. Before that point, Mary worked outside the home at different jobs, and I managed the business and did all of the performing myself. By 1993, when Mary

*Before he learned to walk, Harry had several play stations in the office. Mary made time during her work day for stories, diapers, and playtime—conveniences she wouldn't have enjoyed if she didn't work from home.*

was pregnant, my business had grown so much that I needed outside help so that the phone would be answered in a timely fashion. I was at the point where I was so busy doing jobs, I had little time to hunt for new work or talk to the clients I already had. Mary now handles all of the sales and marketing for my live performances. She also writes articles for several trade magazines. And in the past two years, she's taken on responsibility for editing, advertising and selling our new line of books, videos and newsletters.

It may surprise

you to learn that given this work load, Mary has no outside help caring for our son. In fact, we made it a priority that she be Harry's primary care-giver. The three days Mary spent in the hospital following Harry's birth was the only "maternity leave" she took. How do we manage this?

One of the benefits of entertaining families for a living is that you get to attend cool events and meet lots of interesting characters.

With planning, discipline and love. Ever since he was born, Harry has had a play center in our office. In the beginning, it was a blanket and a few simple toys. As he grew, we added sturdy Fisher Price toys, blocks, and his very own "office". He plays while Mary works. At the age of three, he is now beginning to help out—he puts stamps on envelopes and brings in the mail. Sometimes the two of them come to shows with me, and he carries my cord and microphone into the venue and helps me set up for the show. He thinks helping out is a laugh-riot.

Mary tries to answer every phone call within 2 rings, but the answering machine is always on as a backup, especially during the first year when Harry was nursing and needing a diaper change. He learned young—around 10 months—that he needed to play quietly while Mom is on the phone, and that he should not interrupt a phone call unless he is bleeding. (That rule was bent slightly when he was first learning to use the potty. Now that he does that all by himself, the original rule has been reinstated.) He also stays away from the computer, a rule that will change as he grows older and can be trusted to not delete important files.

Lest you think this sounds like a terrible existence for him, let me assure you that he is a very well-adjusted and happy kid, and we are one of the happiest families you will ever meet. Harry is a very creative kid, and entertains himself very well. The freedom to set her own hours means that Mary can take a morning off if she wants—because she knows that she will get the work done in the evenings after Harry goes to bed. She also gets to choose her work site; she has been known to take proofs of a book or article to the playground so Harry could climb and slide with his friends while she reads manuscripts with a red pencil in hand.

## <u>Three simple rules</u>

Mary maintains that there are three keys to successfully running a business from home are:

1.) Establish boundaries. Harry knows when he can have her undivided attention, and when he cannot interrupt unless it is an emergency.

2.) Maintain a balance. If you're like most people, you want to start a home-based business in order to spend more time with your kids. So do it! We constantly reassess our goals so that we can maintain a healthy family life and a strong business. When Harry was one, we really pushed to book more school shows so that I would be done with my shows by 2:30 or 3 PM and could be home for dinner. I also cut back on the number of birthday parties I was doing because I wanted to be home more on the weekends. This may mean that our business won't enjoy rapid growth during Harry's toddler years. That's OK with us. It's our decision—and since we're in charge here, we know we won't be demoted or fired because we choose to put family first!

3.) Keep the television shut up in a cold and unfriendly upstairs room. Harry watches perhaps 1 hour a month of television.  As a result, he has learned to entertain himself very well, so he doesn't require either of us (or the television) to keep him occupied.

All in all, this plan has worked very well for the three of us.  Harry is a joy.  Mary loves the freedom of working in a home office.  Our marriage is stronger because we are a team in every aspect of our lives.  And our home life is much calmer and more satisfying.

## Creative alternatives

When you're first getting started, it is unlikely that your spouse will come to work for you.  I admit that it would be harder for me to perform, keep the office running, and raise Harry without some outside help.  But it is possible, if you are willing to make the trade-offs and be creative.  You control your schedule, and can schedule shows on weekends and evenings so that your spouse or another relative or friend is available to watch your kids.  Or you can develop a show for nursing homes or schools that allows you to leave for work after your kids are in school and lets you get home in time to meet the bus at the end of the day.

One couple we know performs a juggling act, and they bring their daughter to almost every show they perform.  She either sits and watches them perform, or, if they are working an outdoor festival or event, she plays within view while they work.  I don't know too many performers who do this, but it works for this family.  The three of them travel together and love having the "down time" after shows for family explorations of new cities.  Would this work if you had three or four kids?  I know several older couples who travelled together—touring cross country in a Winnebago.  The husband performed as a solo magician while the wife took care of the business and homeschooled the kids.  When the kids were old enough to supervise themselves, she joined the act as the magician's assistant.

Another man I know worked his 7 year old son into his act. The son is his dad's assistant, and the duo twist balloons at local restaurants. (They both enjoy a free meal every night, too!)

You may not dream of chucking everything and living in a Winnebago, and it may not be possible to work your child into your program. I relate these anecdotes because they prove that you can make it work, if you really want to—regardless of the obstacles.

Sit down and talk with your family. I think they will understand that the trade-offs are worth it. In the long run, you'll have much more freedom than you currently have, but in the short term, they may have to take on additional responsibilities for themselves and for the household. If you keep the lines of communication open, you'll be a successful work at home parent!

## Maintaining balance

When your office is in your home, it is easy to lose your priorities. If you have high-needs kids (or a high needs spouse!) who need your undivided attention during their waking hours, you may find yourself burning the candles at both ends so that you can get things done. This is a quick road to burnout.

Procrastination can also add undue stress to your life. When faced with a task you find difficult, such as making cold sales calls or updating your financial records, many home office entrepreneurs make a choice to focus on housework, then wonder why their business isn't successful. Yes, housework needs to get done. But if you're going to work at home successfully, you need to ask yourself every day, "what is the most important thing that needs to be done today." Then you have to do it. Some days, it will be scrubbing the toilet, I promise! Running a business is fun, but it does require some determination and discipline. Mary and I both make lists to help us manage our time. We also share in the household work and cooking.  To make life easier when one of us is on a deadline, we compare schedules so that the necessary household maintenance can be done at a time when it won't disturb a major project.  Or the spouse who isn't on deadline gives Harry a bath and gets him ready for bed while the other spouse works for an extra few minutes in peace and quiet.

As an example, I will put off vacuuming if Mary is on a deadline and trying to get her column written  for *LaughMakers* magazine.  And she will take Harry with her and go work at a friend's house or at the park if I am developing a new show and need a block of time to rehearse without interruptions.

## Making time for fun

Now that the business is a full-time proposition for both of us, we schedule long weekends off once every couple of months so that we can get away from the business and relax as a family (or as a couple, which is equally important!)  We didn't do this in the beginning, because we needed to work most weekends in order to keep the business growing.  But now that we have reached a level of success that supports our family comfortably, we've recognized that it's important to get away from the business from time to time in order to keep our marriage, our family, and our business fresh and creative.

# Chapter 23 • Typical price ranges for New England venues.

This chapter doesn't really fit in anywhere, but I think it's important to include it as an inticement and a frame of reference.

These are the price ranges for solo presenters in particular venues in the New England area for 1997. Fees in your area will no doubt vary, perhaps dramatically. Use the skills you've learned in the earlier chapters of this book to determine competitive fees for your area.

## Elementary schools

You need to do a 45 minute curriculum centered presentation. The single show rate with an audience cap of 200 students is $250—$450. Storytellers get the low end, science or math assembly programs with lots of cool demonstrations get the high end.  Additional shows on the same day at the same school are usually $75 to $200 apiece.

Elementary school after school programs bring performers in to teach a "class" one day a week for at least four weeks.  These usually pay between $50—$75 per class.  Some pay much more if they get loads of grant money.

## Preschools

They like a thirty to forty minute music or circus arts variety show.  $100-$225.  The higher end is usually paid only for graduation shows that include the kids and their families.

## Birthdays

A 45-50 minute show will get $75—$150.  An activity program such as a tea party or game leader activity party is slightly less.  Face painters, costumed characters, or balloon benders with no show usually get between $50 and $75.

## Libraries, small museums, Boys and Girls clubs, fraternal organizations

A forty-five minute family fun performance $175—$300.

## Fairs and festivals

A family comedy variety show that's thirty to forty minutes will get $225—$400 or more, depending on your reputation and if you are performing on stage at a good sized festival.  Strolling entertainment is priced by the hour, or by the day.  Day rates are usually around $300.  The more polished performers here charge $85-$150 an hour for strolling.

## Nursing homes, retirement centers

They like forty to fifty minutes of good old fashioned entertainment for which they like to pay $40-$50.  Some larger retirement centers host special occasions like Grandparents Day, and they usually pay $125-$200.

## Malls and large shopping centers

They like shows similar to those enjoyed by fairs and festivals, though you can charge a bit more here. Many malls have "Kids Clubs" and regularly need entertainers throughout the year, mostly during school vacations and back to school sale days. $250—$400+, again depending on the expected audience size and your name recognition.

## Corporate family day picnics and holiday parties

They want forty five minutes of high energy skills which are funny for the whole family. Sometimes all they want is "walk around entertainment" which is just like busking, but you're working for an hourly rate rather than tips. Most venues pay between $150—$300 for the first show, with large multi-show discounts for the extra hours of strolling or balloon twisting.

## Restaurants

Places where families eat will sometimes let you stroll making balloons or doing bits of magic—for tips. Others pay similar to birthday prices for a couple of hours of table hopping.

# What's next?

Now that you have taken a peek behind the curtains into the real world of kid shows, what did you think? Are you going to use this book as a springboard or a doorstop? Did you catch yourself murmuring, "*I could do that*"? Did you tell a friend, "I've been reading this book that talks about how I can make money by entertaining kids—and I think I'm going to try it!"? Have images of <u>your</u> perfect program flashed through your mind?

I want you to do it. Really! And I want you to get started right now. Plan for one short event sometime soon. Because only then will you begin to realize what a great business this is. There are a lot of us out here who find this a wonderful way to have fun, work for people we like and make darn good money. How many people do you know who can say that about their jobs? Why don't you join the party? Why don't you go back to school? Why not check yourself in to a nursing home? Maybe I'll see you at the country fair or convention center.

Please, don't be like those other folks who get fired

up only to fizzle out. I'm sure you've met people like that. They set their goals and expectations way too high. They drown in a sea of procrastination and want to be perfect before they get started. Let me tell you up front, those negative traits will pop your balloon faster than any earnest attempt to get started ever will. If ever there was a business where perfection was not a requirement, this is it.

With this book I've given you a shove but it's your job to keep peddling and to set the destination for your trip. Do you want to work at parties, schools, libraries, parks, fairs, or any of the other venues we talked about in this book? Choose ONE and go for it. Choose wisely based on your interests, experience, talents and those skills you currently possess. Take your time, make friends along the way and *have fun*. That's what we're paid for!

# Communicating with the Author

Keith Johnson welcomes your communication. We'd love to hear about your experiences as you launch your new business! Your examples and success stories may be included in future editions of this book. To contact Keith Johnson, it is best to write to: Keith Johnson, 25 Wildwood Avenue, Providence, RI 02907. If speed is important, fax to us at (401) 781-7964.

Keith performs over 500 shows a year at venues including schools, libraries, malls, festivals, and corporate family days. His programs: *Science Isn't Always Pretty*, *Amazing Americans*, *I Feel Good!*, *Let's Talk Trash*, *Hats Off to Reading*, and *Just for the Fun of It!* entertain and educate elementary school aged children and their families.

He is the author of *GET YOUR SHOW ON THE ROAD, CREATING AND PERFORMING ROUTINES FOR FAMILY AUDIENCES, WHAT SUCCESSFUL PERFORMERS KNOW, and PROGRESS REPORTS.*

Keith and his wife Mary live in Rhode Island with their son, Harry and three dogs, Doogle, Dexter and Emma.

Keith also consults with others who are in the family entertainment business. For information and a fee schedule, call Mary at (401) 781-6676.

# —FREE—
## Consulting Coupon
## ($25 Consultation Value)

It's impossible for me to cover every question you may have about making money entertaining kids in this book. Let me help you get past your creating, selling, or presenting roadblocks so you can get your business up and running. If you have something you'd like to ask—this is your chance. This certificate entitles you to send <u>one</u> question, comment, observation, vexation, problem, stumbling block or curiousity as it relates to starting a business entertaining kids and families. Be as specific as possible. I am happy to help and interested to hear what's on your mind.

Name_____

Address_____

City, State, Zip_____

Phone_____

Fax_____

E-Mail_____

**Allow 2-4 weeks—by mail or fax only—
no confidentiality guaranteed**

**Send to: Keith Johnson Educational Programs
25 Wildwood Avenue
Providence, RI 02907**

No need to tear out this page. Make a copy, and send it in!

# How Many Shows Do You Do A Year?

Is it as many as you'd like? If not, you need *Get Your Show on the Road*. Whether you're a juggler, magician, clown, balloon bender, or puppeteer, and whether you're a novice or an experienced professional, this book helps you:

• **Write a Show.** Use the easy step-by-step exercises to develop individual routines and weave those routines into a complete show.

•**Find an Audience.** Every show isn't right for every audience. Learn how to choose the best audience for your show, and how to pursue shows in those markets.

•**Deal with Troublemakers.** Kids can enjoy your show without going bonkers. *Get Your Show on the Road* helps you keep your audience in line without being a heavy.

## Here's What Others Have to Say about <u>GET YOUR SHOW ON THE ROAD</u>

*Keith Johnson has written a very honest book, and his principles can be applied to any variety arts performer, whether you're a magician, clown, ventriloquist, juggler or chalk talk artist. The book will give you practical ideas and make you think.*

*—Samuel Patrick Smith*
*Magician and Publisher*

*This book should become the bible for performers every-where. If I had this book 65 years ago, I would have saved time and trouble. And I probably would have become a big star!*

*—Fred Marco Foshey*
*Magician*
*Order of Merlin—Excalibur*

<u>*To order direct from the publisher, call (800) 730-6676 or ask for it at a bookstore near you.*</u>

*Get Your Show on the Road, 224 pages, softcover*
*Publisher: KMJ Educational Programs, 25 Wildwood Avenue, Providence, RI 02907 (800) 730-6676.*
*ISBN 1-890833-01-0*

**Don't let the business of show business get you down!** *Progress Reports* offer simple, easily understood tips for performers who are new to the field, or who want to improve their business skills. Whether you're a clown, magician, puppeteer, face painter, animal act, or juggler, Keith explains issues important to you in simple, clear language.

*Progress Reports* are $8 each, or 3 for $20. As of June 1, 1997, the following Progress Reports are available. We're adding new ones all the time, so for a complete list, please call (800) 730-6676, or e-mail us at keithbooks@aol.com.

**#1. YOU'RE BOOKED!** The best, sure fire, low-cost ways to get bookings fast when you're just starting out in the kid show business. A quick start guide that will make your phone ring, and your wallet happy!

**#2. SETTING FEES.** Hesitant to break into new markets because you don't know what to charge? This is the booklet for you. A no-nonsense guide that helps full-time, part-time and hobby presenters determine what their show is worth. Discover the range of fees in your community, how to determine where you fit in, when (or if) you should negotiate, and how to overcome price resistance from a customer.

**#3 BE A TAX SMART PERFORMER.** Losing sleep because your shoe-box is overflowing with faded receipts? Learn to perform as well for the IRS as you do in your shows. Tips help you keep good records, find frequently overlooked deductions, and more. Real-life advice can minimize your audit risks and help you sleep better at night!

*Progress Reports prices are subject to change without notice. Available by mail only. To order, call (800) 730-6676.*

# What makes successful performers tick?

Performers and presenters from all over America tell how they manage to make money (and have a lot of fun) doing what they love. Whether you dream about performing or live the dream every day, this book will stir your mind and keep you motivated.

WHAT SUCCESSFUL PERFORMERS KNOW is overflowing with real life examples, insights and some secrets of veteran ventriloquists, scientists, actors, magicians, clowns, comedians, historians, jugglers, storytellers, mimes, and more.

Discover—

- •how they got started
- •what they're doing now
- •who inspires them
- •what makes them successful
- •where they're going next

Forty two presenters responded to Keith Johnson's questionnaire about showmanship, creativity, and business. Their words are right here! Learn from the best in WHAT SUCCESSFUL PERFORMERS KNOW.

To order direct from the publisher, call (800) 730-6676. Or ask at a bookstore near you.

*What Successful Performers Know by Keith Johnson*
*96 pages, softcover*
*ISBN 1-890833-04-5*

# Here's What Others Have Said About Keith Johnson

"According to past performers, we have a more difficult audience. Keith handled them with ease. He's very professional and has a great ability for keeping the children's attention."

Kebby Willard, Natick Mall, Natick, MA

"Keith's show was great. He talked to the level of the kids and his humor was easily understood by them. He showed respect for them, which I feel is important."

Donna Bielaczyc, Mark Twain Library, Redding, CT

"The staff at Charlton Street School felt that Keith's program was the best we have had all year—down to earth, at the children's level, funny and educational."

Frank Giardiello, Charlton Street School, Southbridge, MA

"Keith is worth every penny!"

Jean Shaughnessy, Athol Public Library, Athol, MA

"We have never seen a show as original as Keith's program. Keith was very good and spoke to the children at their level. They were never bored, and no one fidgeted. BRAVO!"

Sheila Gellen Gross, Booth Free School, Roxbury, CT

"Keith is one of the best ever! It's not easy to grab the attention of 85 excited kids in Halloween costumes, but Keith had them fascinated and engaged."

Leslie McDonough, Tyler Free Library, Foster, RI

"Keith is a total professional and his performances draw the attention of all types of audiences."

Annamaria Mann, Pawtucket Jaycess, Pawtucket, RI